Reclaiming Bar/Bat Mitzvah

as a Spiritual Rite of Passage

Rabbi Goldie Milgram

Also Available From Reclaiming Judaism Press

MITZVAH CARDS: One Mitzvah Leads to Another

Mitzvah Stories: Seeds for Inspiration and Learning

Seeking & Soaring: Jewish Approaches to Spiritual Direction

Books from Jewish Lights Publishing
by Rabbi Goldie Milgram

Reclaiming Judaism as a Spiritual Practice: Holy Days and Shabbat

Meaning & Mitzvah: Daily Practices for Reclaiming Judaism
through Prayer, God, Torah, Hebrew, Mitzvot & Peoplehood

Living Jewish Life Cycle: How to Create Meaningful
Jewish Rites of Passage at Every Stage of Life

Reclaiming Bar/Bat Mitzvah as a Spiritual Rite of Passage

©2014 Second Edition Goldie Milgram
First published by Jossey-Bass, a Wiley Imprint under the title
Make Your Own Bar/Bat Mitzvah: A Personal Approach to Creating a Meaningful Rite of Passage

Reclaiming Judaism Press
www.Bmitzvah.org & www.ReclaimingJudaism.org

Reclaiming Judaism books can be order through most booksellers and are usually available on Kindle/e-book readers, as well.

Readers should be aware that Internet websites used within might have changed or disappeared between when the book was written and when it is read.

The Library of Congress has catalogued the earlier edition as follows:

Milgram, Goldie, date.
Make your own bar/bat mitzvah: a personal approach to creating a meaningful rite of passage / Goldie Milgram.

p. cm.

ISBN 0-7879-7215-0
1. Bar mitzvah—Handbooks, manuals, etc. 2. Bar mitzvah—Handbooks, manuals, etc. I. Title
MB707.2.M55 2004
296.4'424—dc22 2004005686

Second Edition ISBN:
978-0-9848048-3-2 (pbk, Trade Edition)
978-0-9848048-5-6 (hbk, Library Binding)
978-0-9848048-4-9 (electronic, e-book)

Cover Photo: Neil Heilpern
Book Design: Taylor Rozek

Reclaiming Judaism Press is a subsidiary of the 501C3 non-profit
P'nai Yachadut-Reclaiming Judaism
17 Rodman Oval, New Rochelle, NY 10805
914-500-5696

Printed in the United States of America

Contents

Introduction   9

1   Reclaiming Bar/Bat Mitzvah as a Rite of Initiation   19

2   Developing Your Bar/Bat Mitzvah Action Plan (BMAP)   31

3   Incorporating Awareness, Talents & Interests   51

4   Shaping a Meaningful Jewish Study Plan & Service   79

5   Step-by-Step Guide to Giving a Great D'var Torah   117

6   Exploring Mitzvah Project Options   153

7   Joyful Jewishing: Approaches to Celebrating   171

8   Contemplating Heartfelt Blessings, Gifts & Memories   195

Glossary: Transliterations & Translations   209

Acknowledgements   225

Index   227

Visit Bmitzvah.org: Bibliography, Blog, Books & Resources

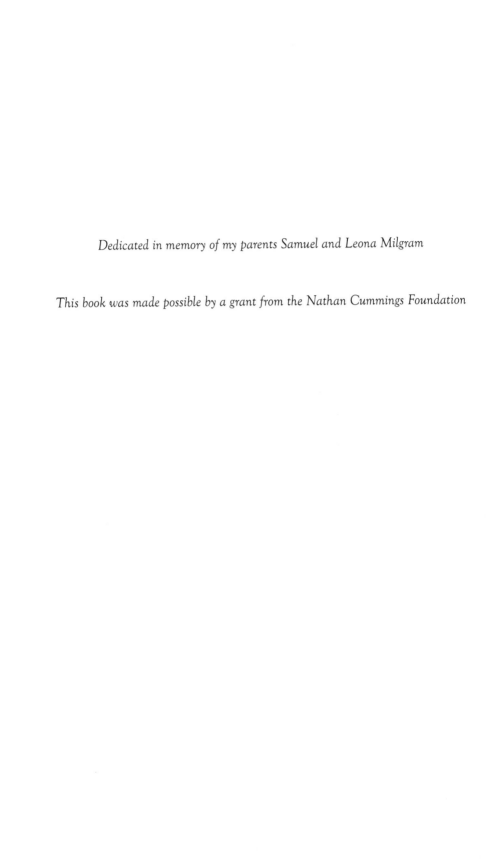

Dedicated in memory of my parents Samuel and Leona Milgram

This book was made possible by a grant from the Nathan Cummings Foundation

Introduction

Are you looking for ways to make the experience of becoming *Bar/Bat Mitzvah* (B-Mitzvah) more meaningful, creative, and spiritual? You have found your source, an empowering guide to help you take charge of the B-Mitzvah process. Our goal is to help you plan a B-Mitzvah that will be both meaningful and memorable for everyone involved—the B-Mitzvah student, family, teachers, tutors, and friends.

What an exciting time in Jewish history to become a B-Mitzvah! It is now possible for you to customize the preparation process, ritual, and celebration. In our view the student's talents, abilities, and interests are a gift to the Jewish people. Just as each person is different, so can every B-Mitzvah have its own personality, creative rituals, and unique characteristics. Rather than a boring time, this can be a time of soaring. Whether you are doing this as a youth or adult B-Mitzvah, independently or in the context of an existing congregation, this book will help you discover how this highly acclaimed, ancient initiation ritual can become the basis for a season of tremendous growth and accomplishment.

This book is based on Rabbi Goldie Milgram's extensive creative research, funded by the Nathan Cummings Foundation, with students, teachers, and families from across the full spectrum of Judaism. She will guide you through a process that turns B-Mitzvah into a fascinating adventure. For families, her methods transform parents from taskmasters into team members supporting an excited and motivated student to fulfill his or her chosen B-Mitzvah goals and dreams. Detailed guidance for B-Mitzvah preparation and planning is provided here for both youth and adult B'nei Mitzvah (the plural of the term).

Before we begin, here is a brief chapter-by-chapter introduction to the creation of a meaningful and memorable B-Mitzvah.

Chapter One
Reclaiming Bar/Bat Mitzvah as a Rite of Initiation

Becoming B-Mitzvah is a process that involves preparation of a student for initiation into a satisfying and responsible Jewish life. A healthy initiation process has several key elements that help students to develop as people and as skillful members of their "tribe." This chapter contrasts the steps of B-Mitzvah preparation with the classic components of initiation practices of other cultures. This brief study will clarify the full power and potential of B-Mitzvah. It also reviews the surprising origins of B-Mitzvah, a practice not found in the Torah.

Support for personal development and a vision of how each student's uniqueness is a gift to our people is also part of this initiation process. B-Mitzvah students are meant to come to know themselves better, to identify how they want to express their coming of age as Jews, to learn to experience life as a journey, and to learn to use tribal practices as a source of inspiration for living. By undertaking instruction in the skills needed to accomplish difficult tasks and carrying them out, candidates establish their readiness for greater autonomy and learn that they are worthy of their people's trust.

Chapter Two
Developing Your Bar/Bat Mitzvah Action Plan (BMAP)

The process of creating a B-Mitzvah Action Plan (BMAP) increases enthusiasm, reduces conflict, facilitates cooperation, and expands the vision of what is possible. Our planning guide helps each person directly involved to become clear about his or her goals for this special occasion, and provides an enjoyable process and helpful tools for family and friends who are part of the B-Mitzvah planning team.

This section also offers many examples and suggestions to help support and stimulate your own creative thinking. By setting your goals in the first three essential dimensions of ritual planning—emotional, intellectual, and spiritual—and only then determining the physical dimension (the logistics necessary to meet your goals), your decisions will result in an amazingly satisfying and unique B-Mitzvah. Those who go through this process come to recognize themselves as essential to making the hoped-for holiness and happiness happen, because this planning process clarifies each person's hopes, roles, and responsibilities.

Chapter Three
Incorporating Awareness, Talents & Interests

Every human being is a gift to the community. No one else has your exact design, life experience, family traditions, generational legacy, talents, and ideas. On the day of becoming B-Mitzvah, the student steps forward as a teacher, thinker, and leader of the Jewish future. This is a powerful experience for both youth and adult B-Mitzvah students. Family and friends get a new look at who the student is becoming. This helps family and community to give the greater autonomy that a young adult will naturally begin to seek. Male and female alike, adult B-Mitzvah students also have the joy of manifesting in community, in the fullness of their expanded Jewish ritual skills, knowledge of Torah and opportunity to harvest and share inner wisdom.

This chapter helps to inventory the B-Mitzvah student's strengths and interests. Through this process a person learns the language of his or her spirit. What is the student good at? What is she interested in? Interests provide useful metaphors for teaching Torah and thinking about life. For some it is sports—making a home run, being in the zone; for others it is music, politics, crafts, environmentalism, pets, or computers. Here one's uniqueness is revealed as an important B-Mitzvah asset.

The inner circle of your life is composed of the people who will show up when you need someone to help, care, or listen and those for whom you will show up when they are similarly in need. This is a very important concept. In Judaism the quorum of ten required for prayer services is called a *minyan*. We use the term the *minyan* of your life to go beyond those whom you pray with to include the inner circle of people in your life who will help you prepare, listen with all their hearts to what you have to teach them, and celebrate your accomplishments. Because these are the people to have in mind during this preparation process, this chapter also helps the student to assess who really is in your inner circle and to contemplate how to expand that circle of support for the journey called life.

Chapter Four
Shaping a Meaningful Jewish Study Plan & Service

We all need and deserve a far deeper understanding of Judaism than is offered in most conventional religious schools. This book offers an introduction to the deeper, more meaningful and spiritual waters of Judaism.

You are fortunate to be alive during a time of Jewish spiritual renaissance. No longer is there reason to recite prayers by rote. We are recovering the meaning and power of prayers and practices that the trauma of the Holocaust had buried. Bring your hopes, curiosity, and questions to this chapter to learn the skills for finding meaning in Jewish prayers and practices.

If it is at all feasible, we recommend that B-Mitzvah preparations be conducted over an eighteen-month to two-year period. This greatly reduces stress, tension, and performance anxiety. The transformations in a young person during such an interval are particularly stunning. For parents, siblings, friends, teachers, and the student, to do B-Mitzvah well is a phenomenal experience.

In this chapter you will learn answers to questions such as, Why are there two Shabbat candles? Why are they white? Why is Shabbat (the Sabbath) called a bride? Why bother with *tallit, kippah,* or *tephillin?* Is there significance to the order of the prayers in services? Why does *Kaddish* seem to be so important to people? And can a service really be made meaningful and interesting?

You can often have a lot of influence over your B-Mitzvah service. This book will put power into your hands because we will show you how the Shabbat morning service fits together. Services are full' of hidden spiritual nutrients, and here you will learn how to take them in. Many communities encourage B-Mitzvah families to create a booklet of readings or a creative service, so we will also provide you with a guide to customizing the service for your special day. Because Judaism teaches that life is a spiritual journey, this chapter offers several stimulating models for mentoring in the issues of daily life as well.

Chapter Five
Step-by-Step Guide to Giving a Great D'var Torah

On B-Mitzvah day the student steps up to the pulpit as a leader of the Jewish people by having discovered messages within her Torah portion that her spirit knows she must bring to the community's attention. That's what a revelation is, when something important is revealed. The prophets used passion and poetry to communicate. How will the student's message get across? It doesn't have to be through a speech. Self-expression can also take the form of creating a website, poetry, a song, a ballad, a dance, a play, paintings, and more.

Before deciding what method of teaching to choose comes a period of seeking meaning for living from within your Torah portion. This chapter offers many tools to help you discover inspiring messages that are not at first apparent when reading the Torah. We've included a variety of approaches because people have differing learning styles. Once you acquire the ability to find meaning in a Torah portion, then it becomes possible to *shema* (listen) and learn from Torah for the rest of your life. This is one of the hidden gifts in the B-Mitzvah process.

A big shift happens when teaching Torah on B-Mitzvah day. The most important thing is not telling people what the portion means to you; it is helping those present connect to what the Torah portion might offer for them; this is leadership, and reveals what it means to become a teacher. We'll show you how to do this—and you will shine.

Chapter Six
Exploring Mitzvah Project Options

Judaism encourages practices that bring healing and holiness into the world. Our expression for such a practice is *making a mitzvah*. There are 194 positive mitzvot (honor parents, help those in need, live in awe) and 77 negative ones (don't embarrass people, don't murder...). Judaism is designed to help a person connect to life with awe and respect. The practices of Judaism are designed to give a person the energy and enthusiasm to live a mitzvah-centered existence.

Those who mentor B-Mitzvah students have among their goals the nurturing of empathy and social action. Crossing the threshold not only makes the student into a teacher, it also means cultivating the ability to take care of yourself and others. B-Mitzvah students can explore their own power to make a mitzvah happen by creating and implementing a plan to create positive change in the world through their own determined actions. This chapter reveals spiritual meanings for many of the mitzvot and will help each student to find a mitzvah challenge to take on as part of the initiation process.

Chapter Seven
Joyful Jewishing: Approaches to Celebrating

Right in Jewish law you can read that it is a mitzvah to hold a *seudah shel mitzvah*, a meal for the guests who have come to witness the B-mitzvah ritual and celebrate this joyous occasion. *Hiddur* mitzvah is Hebrew for the Jewish principle that it is spiritual to beautify a mitzvah—and so beautifying the party is also a mitzvah. This includes designing a beautiful invitation, wearing lovely new clothes, having special music, creating a wonderful environment, and concluding with attractive notes of appreciation. Or it could mean holding the ritual in Israel, using products from Israel, honoring the B-Mitzvah student through a donation in her name to a charity, commissioning new Jewish art to make your celebration more special, and much more.

From your B-Mitzvah Action Plan (BMAP) evaluation of personal strength and depth of Torah study will emerge certain key values and ideas you intend to communicate to those who come to the B-Mitzvah service and celebration. This chapter reveals the power of having a meaningful Jewish theme that can flow through the entire experience and so strengthen the beauty and power of the day. Our guide to finding your own theme will bring many interesting possibilities to the surface and launch you into party planning in a remarkable way.

In this chapter we will also look at how to create an atmosphere conducive to holiness and joy. We will offer guidance in the importance of forging firm understandings on role and timing with photographers and party planners, as they may not be familiar with some of the beautiful nuances the BMAP process can inspire.

Chapter Eight
Contemplating Heartfelt Blessings, Gifts & Memories

To honor family, friends, teachers, and mentors both alive and deceased during the B-Mitzvah process is to give them a gift. This chapter will help you decide whom to honor and what to say. It will offer many Jewishly profound and authentic ways to create powerful moments that sincerely honor the inner circle of the student's life.

The gifts a person will receive from guests also benefit from reflection. This chapter offers a giver's guide that families might want to share with elders, close friends, classmates, and others of significance to you. In addition to exploring the tradition of giving to a worthy cause in honor of a life-cycle accomplishment, the guide also helps readers explore the power of giving heirlooms and creating moments of legacy and blessing between the giver and recipient.

Writing thank-you notes has traditionally been the last act of the B-Mitzvah student's ritual process. Learning the art of reflecting on life as a spiritual journey is a step that mentors can take to help bring closure to this remarkable season in a family's life. Taking a further step holds tremendous value: a reunion of your B-Mitzvah planning team, from a week to a year later, to reflect upon the entire experience together. This section concludes by providing questions and methods for an enjoyable and effective harvesting of your B-Mitzvah experience.

A Note On Hebrew And Pronunciation

All of the Hebrew expressions in this book are transliterated to make it easier for you to pronounce words comfortably and authentically. The sound of Hebrew is beautiful, powerful, and poetic. Hebrew does not have certain sounds that English does; for example, there is no "th" as in "this" or "j" as in "juice" or "ch" as in "change." Whenever you see a "ch" letter in a transliteration, it is meant to be pronounced gutturally, like a "kh" sound, as though you are clearing your throat. In the Glossary at the end of the book, words are not only carefully and clearly defined but their pronunciations are even more specifically laid out, along with notes about regional and Yiddish variations in pronunciation.

How To Use This Book

Note: If organizing the party is an immediate pressure for you, go read that chapter now. There are exciting possibilities worth knowing about before you make any irrevocable financial commitments.

Primarily we recommend that you and your B-Mitzvah support team read each chapter once over lightly and then begin again, going through the book more carefully in order to undertake the planning opportunities in depth. Consider asking close relatives, clergy, tutors, and siblings to read along, too. Because prior generations may not have had very satisfying B-Mitzvah experiences, this book can be helpful for opening hearts to exciting new possibilities. The material in this book was tested with a wide range of individuals and communities and proven to greatly enhance enthusiasm for the B-Mitzvah process, depth of learning, and creativity.

Those who have been through B-Mitzvah will tell you, as we've mentioned, to begin planning well in advance. By setting aside precious time to fully set up this remarkable process, you'll get back far more than most any other activity to which you might have allocated your time. Through this comprehensive approach to B-Mitzvah, you will have embarked upon a most memorable spiritual adventure. This process can greatly increase the ability of all involved to appreciate and practice Judaism and to navigate life's opportunities and challenges.

Let's get started! Chapter One sets you on the path of understanding the essential roots of the B-Mitzvah experience as a process of preparation for initiation into a satisfying and responsible Jewish life.

Chapter One

Reclaiming Bar/Bat Mitzvah as a Rite of Initiation

What defines a successful *Bar/Bat Mitzvah* (B-Mitzvah)? Before we get to the logistics—location, entertainment, food, decorations—it is important to talk about the most important hopes and dreams you have for the event. Let's consider the underlying purpose and elements needed to achieve emotional satisfaction, as well as the spiritual, philosophical, and perhaps political goals that are important to your identity as a Jew.

Even in the business world, before determining a strategic plan a company must develop a mission statement, principles of operation, goals, and objectives. By defining goals and expectations at this point, you can prevent disappointment and chaos by establishing the clarity and mutual understanding needed to sustain a joyful, thought-provoking, and satisfying experience for all who are involved.

So first let's consider the basic definition of what the B-Mitzvah was originally intended to be.

So What's A Mitzvah?

A *mitzvah*, commonly known as a commandment, is an act done with consciousness that increases (w)holiness in the world. Ideally, a person who is preparing for B-Mitzvah is becoming experienced in how to live a healthy, mitzvah-centered Jewish life and as of age thirteen is considered to no longer require parental supervision of his or her practice of Judaism. So achieving B-Mitzvah means basically that an individual is at the point in life where he or she can take on personal responsibility for performing the *mitzvot* (plural of the term).

Many mitzvot apply only at particular times of life or to certain situations. It's only theoretically possible to practice all of the mitzvot; after all, we're only human. The idea today is to know about them, try them on gradually, and grow into them when they make sense for your life. Major mitzvah categories include the following:

Holidays: These expand the meaning of being alive by focusing our attention on principles such as freedom (Passover), care of and gratitude for our ecosystem (Sukkot), and the right to abstain from work (Shabbat). Holiday mitzvot season our days with a culture rich in flavors, sacred music and stories, the history of our ancient people, and practices that help us to build a better self and strengthen family and community.

Life-cycle events: These peak transitions are occasions for gathering the inner circle of your life for rituals of support, reflection, dedication, and commemoration or celebration.

Justice and peoplehood: The Torah charges us with the duty of pursuing justice, engaging in deeds of loving-kindness, and maintaining compassion for all. We have mitzvot that teach us to care for the safety, health, culture, and wellbeing of our people, all people, the land of Israel, the planet, and all countries in which we dwell.

Study: Challenges faced by our early ancestors on the journey called life and the wisdom they gained along the way are embedded within the Torah and its many subsequent commentaries. Judaism, one of the world's most ancient and ever-evolving wisdom traditions, emphasizes the mitzvah of sacred text study and that of adding your vision, views, and values to the chain of transmitted insight-for-living that has been maintained unbroken through the thousands of years of our people's existence.

Prayer: Through the prayer on the page and the prayer of your heart, Jewish prayer practices nourish the human spirit in matters of gratitude, pain, loss, despair, and love. Our prayer services and rituals, when understood, result in a restoration of energy, support for healing, and infusion of joy for living.

So these are some of the most important tasks and responsibilities of a Jew. Altogether there are 613 mitzvot. We fulfill some by conscious passivism, meaning that what you don't do is what counts: for example, not stealing, murdering, or engaging in false advertising. Many mitzvot require positive action, such as teaching a poor person a trade, rescuing a hostage, working on relationship problems through a process called *teshuvah*, uniquely shaping the meaning of time and place by lighting Shabbat and Yizkor (memorial) candles or the Hanukkah *menorah*, sitting in a sukkah, witnessing the reading of the Torah, and visiting Israel, and much more. Some of the 613 mitzvot are no longer relevant, such as those from the sacrificial system of long ago.

The Earliest B-Mitzvah

Perhaps you will be surprised to learn that the Torah never mentions *Bar Mitzvah*. Keep in mind that the story of Abraham dates around 1200-1300 B.C.E. The term *Bar Mitzvah* is first documented in the eighth century C.E. Evidence reveals that a form of *Bat Mitzvah* was offered in Germany beginning in 1814, then in the Balkans and Italy by the mid-1800s, in Cairo by 1907, and in the United States in 1921. A number of countries have just begun to understand the importance of celebrating the commitment across the full spectrum of gender; the Jewish community in Romania has only just adopted *Bat Mitzvah*.

It seems that in its early stages a *Bar Mitzvah* ritual was not done by the young man but rather by his father! Having labored to raise a committed and knowledgeable son, a parental ritual emerged of publicly reciting a blessing for having become free of the responsibility to supervise his relationship to the mitzvot. Some parents still choose to offer this blessing: *Baruch she-petarani mei-onsho shel zeh*, "Blessed is the one who has exempted me from the punishment of this one." Today's denominational prayer books offer a range of alternative blessings that reflect changing perspectives on the meaning of B-Mitzvah. Many parents and students also choose to add the blessing known as the *Shehecheyanu*, which expresses gratitude to the Source for "giving us life, sustaining us and bringing us to this season."

Many of the rituals and requirements associated with B-Mitzvah today would be quite surprising to those who first introduced the concept. This is because each generation interprets and evolves the wisdom and practices that nourish and guide the life of our people. Indeed, we have a practice called *hiddur* mitzvah, "the beautification" of a mitzvah. It is in itself a mitzvah to improve, advance, glorify, decorate, and expand the meaning, practice, and quality of the many mitzvot. So our tradition encourages and supports each of us in the quest to reflect the unique content of our individual lives during B-Mitzvah rituals and celebration.

Finding Universal Ritual Elements Across Cultures

Why is thirteen the minimum age traditionally associated with B-Mitzvah? In order to connect this practice to the Torah, an ancient story-style form of Torah commentary known as *midrash* is used to assess thirteen as the age of Abraham when he rejected the idol worship of his father, Terach. Thirteen is also considered to be the age of the biblical artist Bezalel, who fashioned the elaborately decorated tabernacle that the Israelites carried through the wilderness. Additionally, sources from various periods of Jewish history suggest that twelve, twelve and a half, and thirteen plus one day are when a person's vows (promises) are considered binding upon them; before that age Jewish law would require approval of a responsible adult. Some communities offer age twelve plus

The Shaman, The Bar Mitzvah Student & The Rabbi

Note from Rabbi Milgram: When my son Mark was twelve, he and I had a very significant chance encounter with a shaman, a Native American healer, in a museum of native peoples on Victoria Island, off the coast of Vancouver, Canada. What happened dramatically advanced our understanding of *Bar Mitzvah* as a rite of initiation and raises important considerations.

I felt a tap on my shoulder as Mark and I walked into the native people's museum and into a crowded room filled with glass cases lined with colorful, carved wooden animal masks.

"Is that your son?" inquired a man wearing a multitoothed fish jaw on a leather thong around his neck atop his red plaid flannel shirt. A museum guide nametag pinned to his lapel identified him: Pachi, Native Docent.

"Yes," I answered.

"Are you a Jewish shaman?" inquired the tribal representative.

I paused before responding, thinking that he must be asking because of my head covering, called a *yarmulke* (Yiddish) or *kippah* (Hebrew). My son had noticed us and answered: "Mom? Yeah, she is, more or less. We're Jewish, and we call our shamans rabbis."

The docent turned to my son and said: "I've heard the puberty rituals of your people are very special. Would you tell me about yours?"

Mark turned crimson, then wisely responded in his newly cracking voice: "Um, would you tell me about yours first?"

Pachi, who was middle-aged and had a weathered and kindly face, began by saying: "A person's most important possessions in this world are your names, your song, your dances, and your masks. These are how you will be remembered when you are gone; these are how you pass on the wisdom of your life; and this is the most important inheritance a person can leave."

Pachi reverentially caressed a mask that he identified as his father's. Lifting the red, green, and white raptor head carving to set atop his own head, he became the story of an agile scout, covering miles and miles filled with adventures. His gestures showed the missions were very serious; they must result in sighting food for the tribe. The dance was a powerful transmission of the skills of a scout.

Mark was fascinated. He inquired further, using the analytical method common to Jewish text study, revealing that he had noticed something curious about the opening statement: "Mr. Pachi, you said 'dances,' 'masks,' 'names.' Those are plural, so why only 'song' and not 'songs'?"

Pachi continued: "Mark, let's say you belong to my tribe. The first verse of the song of your own life you must write during the year of age twelve. How to do this is an art communicated by a mentor. This mentor will be chosen from a different family than your own. If you are a boy, your first mentor will be a man. He will help you look back on your young life and think about the hard times, special times, joyful and suecessful times. From this reflection will come the first verse of your song.

"You will add a verse at age twenty, and thirty and fifty, if you live that long, and at your marriage and the birth of your children, sometimes also if you survive a dramatically dangerous thing. You will sing your first verse at your puberty feast and at that time wear your first mask, dance your father's dances, and then dance one of your own, which you create.".

He paused to reflect and added: "Mark, you will become a mentor too, when you are an adult. A mentor helps you find your place in the tribe, to make sense of your life."

Pachi turned to me and continued: "There must be an economy of words to the song, a splendor to it, and a combination of personal individuality and yet conformity with the metaphors of tribal tradition. It must reflect an integration of the values of the tribe and self-awareness. It is sung softly by your mother should the shaman have to come when you are ill, and it is sung by the tribe at your death. At your death your names will all be spoken and your dances danced with your masks as our way of recalling your life."

Then Pachi asked Mark: "And how about *your* people's coming-of-age rituals?"

ANSWERING PACHI: COMPARING YOURSELF TO THE UNIVERSAL

How would you answer Pachi? This exercise may be helpful in taking a more detailed look at the elements of a traditional initiation ritual and comparing them with the components of contemporary B-Mitzvah. What correspondences do you and your family find between these?

Elements of a Traditional Initiation Ritual	Correspondences with B-Mitzvah
A physical trial or major task that requires focus, skill building, and discipline	
Trainers or mentors, usually from outside the immediate family, help the initiate become skillful, thoughtful, confident, and successful.	
The initiate applies his or her special talents to achieving the task.	
Mentor(s) help the initiate to recognize what is involved in discovering and overcoming obstacles. They convey an understanding of life as a precious journey. The challenges of the preparation process itself become a metaphor for the experience of navigating through life.	
Traditional male and female roles are explained, discussed, and reinforced. The initiate is taught to honor his or her body as a vessel that gives and holds life. Genital marking occurs in some tribes.	
The initiate undertakes a mission that will benefit the tribe or serve the greater good of the land or the gods.	

ANSWERING PACHI: COMPARING YOURSELF TO THE UNIVERSAL

How would you answer Pachi? This exercise may be helpful in taking a more detailed look at the elements of a traditional initiation ritual and comparing them with the components of contemporary B-Mitzvah. What correspondences do you and your family find between these?

Elements of a Traditional Initiation Ritual	Correspondences with B-Mitzvah
Initiates learn traditional practices through which they can gather energy for living. These often involve visioning rituals, expression of the prayer of the heart, and the importance of being part of a group and caring for each other. Often these are taught through experiences that are conducted outdoors and that involve some element of risk or fear.	
A communal ritual is held on a date determined by tradition or when mentor(s) and initiate agree the learning and accomplishments desired have been attained. This decision and ritual is usually facilitated by a shaman, priest, or elder(s).	
The initiate is given space to show leadership, talent, and proficiency in tribal practices. This time of empowered, public, personal leadership can be expressed in many ways, for example, storytelling, a speech, visual arts such as mask making, dance, and music.	
The ritual is preceded by or contained within a religious service that is designed to connect those present to the tribal understanding of the Source(s) of Life. This is done through liturgy, prayer, symbols, song, dance, and the retelling of sacred stories.	*(Continued)*

ANSWERING PACHI: COMPARING YOURSELF TO THE UNIVERSAL	
How would you answer Pachi? This exercise may be helpful in taking a more detailed look at the elements of a traditional initiation ritual and comparing them with the components of contemporary B-Mitzvah. What correspondences do you and your family find between these?	
Elements of a Traditional Initiation Ritual	**Correspondences with B-Mitzvah**
The memory of the ancestors may be invoked.	
The initiate receives or acquires ritual items for communal and personal use. Instruction is given in their applications in daily and festival life, and the initiate puts these into use during the ritual.	
Often the shaman, family members, or friends will sing a tribute to the initiate's qualities and accomplishments.	
A great joyful reception in the full celebratory culture of the tribe (traditional meal rituals, foods, dances, and entertainment) is held in order to host generously those who have attended the ritual and delight in what has transpired.	
Sacrifices, gifts, or donations are dedicated to the Source of Life in appreciation for the youth having reached this significant time.	
Presentations of heartfelt blessings, and ritual actions such as dusting with pollen as a blessing of fertility and giving of gifts heavy with symbolism, are made to the initiate.	

one day as the minimum for *Bat Mitzvah*, also citing earlier maturation of some girls as the rationale. In our time many prefer a minimum age of thirteen for both Bar and *Bat Mitzvah* to emphasize parity between the genders.

Today many adults are also preparing for their own B-Mitzvah because they have only now developed or reclaimed a meaningful connection to Judaism. And most often in the case of women, this ritual was not made available to them in their youth. There is also a tradition of preparing for celebration of a second B-Mitzvah upon attaining the age of eighty-three. Age sixty used to be considered to be a ripe old age prior to the advent of penicillin and modern medicine, so extra years of life afterward are viewed as entry into a second cycle of living. Some individuals have chosen to hold a second B-Mitzvah at an age younger than age eighty-three because of their need to heal from difficulties or disappointments in their original B-Mitzvah.

Virtually all tribal societies develop a rite of initiation for asserting that a person is a talented, educated member of the tribe. Adult B'nei Mitzvah students often contract a talented teacher and form a supportive study group, in addition to selecting private mentors. This process offers tremendous growth as a Jew, pride of accomplishment, and strengthening of your circles of friendship. In the case of an adolescent, a well-designed B-Mitzvah process helps with the age-appropriate shift from focus on self and dependence on others to the capacity for greater personal autonomy and responsible interdependence.

B-Mitzvah As Both Destination And Journey

Has your investigation into B-Mitzvah as a rite of initiation revealed many parallel steps with ritual practices of other ancient cultures? The ritual and party are actually, so to speak, the icing on the cake of a B-Mitzvah. The most important part of becoming B-Mitzvah is what happens on the journey toward the day of the ritual. Who you are is constantly shaped by where you have been, with whom you spend your time, and on what you focus your attention. From now until you become B-Mitzvah, you have a remarkable opportunity to incorporate many delightful, challenging, and meaningful elements into the process of preparation, implementation, and celebration.

Have you explored the hopes and expectations this day holds for yourself, for your family, and for your community? In the next section, our B-Mitzvah Action Plan will help you discover what is needed, and you will likely uncover many precious opportunities to create a remarkable, memorable experience for all involved!

Chapter Two

Developing Your Bar/Bat Mitzvah Action Plan (BMAP)

The next step in preparing your *Bar/Bat Mitzvah* (B-Mitzvah) is to create your B-Mitzvah Action Plan, which we'll call a BMAP. The BMAP is an effective model for ritual planning. It is based upon an ancient Jewish model for understanding religious experience by considering four essential dimensions. When applied to B-Mitzvah, this means you will be planning to support a process that involves

- Emotional satisfaction
- Intellectual expansion
- Spiritual connection
- Logistical excellence

Too often the cart gets before the horse during B-Mitzvah planning; logistics get fixed before dreams and feelings are explored, shared, and transformed into plans. This creates unnecessary losses, which can be prevented by following the BMAP process. When the B-Mitzvah student and immediate family or support team take the time to establish satisfying goals and objectives for each of the first three dimensions, then it is possible to truly determine the logistics necessary for successful implementation. So long as you complete all the dimensions before making final decisions, you can start in any of the dimensions because all of them are happening simultaneously within the event and within the participants. We find it particularly effective to begin with setting emotional goals.

Emotional Satisfaction

Ben and Sara are twins who are having their B-Mitzvahs at the same time. At a family planning session, everyone made a list of the emotions they hoped and expected to feel during the B-Mitzvah preparation process. Each participant then highlighted those emotions that represent their most important emotional goals and emotional concerns.

Some of the emotional goals that appear on Ben's list are "to feel independent, unique, and proud of myself." Among his emotional concerns, he listed "anxiety about public speaking. Sara's list shared Ben's desire for her uniqueness to show through; she also emphasized wanting to "feel connected to family," and she expressed one of her fears as being about the possibility of "hurt feelings." Their dad and mom also had concerns on their list; a shared one was cost.

What kind of objectives might help ensure that these emotional goals and concerns can be met? Here is some of what came up at a family brainstorming session.

Ben and Sara could have different tutors. This way each can learn at
    his or her own style and pace, formulate independent thoughts, and
    have enough contact time to feel prepared and competent. This
    might also help allay Ben's anxiety about public speaking.
Our family could offer an open mike at the reception and allow
    people to tell stories about what they admire and recall about these
    B-Mitzvah students, as well as other family members and friends,
    past and present. The uniqueness of each will be reflected as the
    family lore is told.
Differences create opportunities and often are the focus of prejudice.
    Ben or Sara could develop or join a mitzvah project that helps to

fight prejudice. Although creating social change is a spiritual goal, one practical effect can be a sense of independence where they might form new relationships that expand their world beyond school and family while doing this work.

The stories of sibling pairs in the Torah might be an interesting focus of study. What about the twins Jacob and Esau and the sisters Leah and Rachel? The entire Torah is read in sequential weekly sections each year. Although B-Mitzvah technically happens on one's thirteenth birthday plus one day, the actual ritual can be held at any later point in life. Because Ben and Sara's congregation has more B-Mitzvah students than weeks in the year, maybe their ritual could be on the Shabbat when one of the Torah portions that address Jacob, Esau, Leah, or Rachel will be read.

Sara's mom wonders if Sara, who is a dancer, could offer an interpretive dance about these Torah-based sibling relationships as her unique form of teaching about the Torah portion, since it is customary during the Torah service for the B-Mitzvah initiate to offer an inspiring teaching about the weekly Torah portion, which is called giving a dvar Torah.

Ben plays the guitar and writes songs. If the Torah portion is about Jacob and Esau, maybe Ben could create a ballad about how differences in the nature and abilities of these twins play an important role in the story of the Jewish people. Perhaps singing this could be part of his way of teaching Torah at the B-Mitzvah ritual. King David, Moses, and Kohelet (Ecclesiastes) each offer a shirah (song) in the Torah as a form of prayer and ethical guidance. For Ben to do so would be to connect to those men as role models, and to draw on one of his own strengths, which will help him feel proud of himself.

Note that it is a custom in some congregations for girls to become B-Mitzvah at age twelve. So Sara and Ben might also have different B-Mitzvah dates if that is a strongly held local practice or if the family's process deems it desirable.

Ben could interview people who speak well in public and ask if one of them would coach him for the B-Mitzvah. This way he develops a major life skill and can feel proud at his commitment and preparation.

Sara's desire to foster family closeness reminded everyone of having seen something special at a neighbor's *Bat Mitzvah*. When the Torah's home, the "ark," was opened, a representative from each generation of the family was invited to come up, and starting with the oldest, each passed the Torah until it reached the B-Mitzvah student. This could create a beautiful forum for acknowledging many people and emphasizing how many generations are present.

Their dad remembered that the *Kaddish* prayer, when recited by mourners, can be introduced by inviting those present who desire to take a turn from their seats, to speak aloud the names and qualities of deceased family members and friends who are dearly missed. This would further personalize prayer for their service, and reduce the potential for hurt feelings by increasing the opportunities for more people to feel involved.

Sara's mom remembered being at a *Bar Mitzvah* where family and friends were honored by having the student call up family members for group *aliyot* (the covenantal process of coming up to witness the Torah reading): "Will all of my cousins who have been *bar* or *bat mitzvah* please come up for this *aliyah*," "my Jewish aunts and uncles for the next," "our friends from Camp Ramah are next," and so on. Group aliyot greatly expand the family's ability to offer the honor of an *aliyah* (singular form) and dramatize the categories of people in Ben and Sara's life in a powerfully affirming way.

Sara wondered, "Couldn't the party also offer opportunities for deepening family ties?" and suggested making a family tree booklet to hand out as the party favor. This is a project that makes sure everyone in the family's names are mentioned and starts deepening family ties long before the party because all the contacts necessary to create it must be set into motion long in advance.

As the family's list developed, Ben added one more unifying idea:

The *Havdalah* candle used to conclude Shabbat is braided, so instead of the giant secular birthday cake candle-lighting ritual honoring relatives that the caterers seem to push, we could do a Jewish candle-lighting by celebrating *Havdalah* on Saturday night at the beginning of the party. I could talk about how, like the two separate candles that start Shabbat, Sara and I are very different and yet, like the *Havdalah* candle, we are really braided together in the life of our family. I love to watch Sara when she is dancing and happy. A braid is stronger than each of its single candles—that is what makes the power of family and community.

Sara then added: We could stand in a circle during *Havdalah* and invite everyone from our lives, from every religion and country, to step forward as honored guests by category—friends, relatives, schoolmates, teammates, teachers, mom and dad's co-workers, and those who traveled the farthest to come, and more. We can say how important it is to honor our differences; just as Ben and I are both Jewish and yet very different as individuals, they are very special to us in their own unique ways of being. We can explain that this ritual shows the theme we've found for our B-Mitzvah— how we are all braided together in order to combine our differences and talents to make a more wonderful world.

The family was very excited by this process and shared the results with their rabbi. He was very supportive and interested in their process, although he didn't think every idea would work in their particular congregation. He also contributed an idea for their list: when they meet with the cantor they might ask her to teach them "*Hevdalim*," Rabbi Leila Berner's *Havdalah* song about honoring differences. It might be perfect for their ritual. (This is found in *Shirim Uvrahot*— a slim manual of blessings for home-based Jewish meal-time rituals, with a companion music, available at JRF.org.)

Let's look at what has happened in this process so far:

- Ben and Sara have a team rooting for them.
- The family sees the B-Mitzvah as a both a journey and a goal.
- They are creating shared memories.
- No one feels alone or unsupported in his or her responsibilities; all are in this together.

- The unique talents and interests of the students are supported.
- Once the most pressing hopes and concerns are supported, then each person has the room to notice and support others.
- The rabbi is respectfully included and is happy to learn of the family's process, which lets him contribute in a positive way to the plan.

Ideas in this dimension have triggered necessary or interesting goals for the other dimensions. A holistic idea of a meaningful, exciting B-Mitzvah plan is already beginning to emerge.

But wait a minute, what about the parents' concern about cost? It is important to pause during each dimension and go down everyone's list to make sure their goals have been attended to. We almost missed one. The family's brainstorming led to an agreement to hold a budgeting session and to track and control expenses. This also turned out to be an important part of Ben and Sara's initiation process, as they became part of a team learning about the costs of things, organizing a budget, and monitoring expenses for a major project.

Tip

BMAP to Avoid These Serious Mistakes
Here are some comments that former B-Mitzvah students from a variety of sections of the country and denominations, who are now in graduate school, made about their own B'nei Mitzvah experiences.

Karen
My uncle from Alabama died the year after my B-Mitzvah. I later learned he was a sculptor, an artist, like I want to be. He was actually at my B-Mitzvah and I never met him, or realized I'd have wanted to. Why didn't we have an open mike for people to introduce themselves, to share something of themselves, a song,

a poem, a bit of family history? I was so busy hanging out with classmates I never really met the family, and alas, I was the last person of B-Mitzvah age in our family. I didn't really understand the chance I'd missed until having children of my own.

Tanya

My school has students from many cultures, and it's a lot of fun going to events in each other's families. I've been to a full Chinese wedding, a high-mass Catholic wedding, a Hindu home dedication ritual, and lots more. I was so bummed, my parents hired only a jazz combo for my *Bat Mitzvah* party. I'd always imagined a Klezmer group and a dance teacher on hand to help my friends and guests learn the steps to some of the wild, fast, joyful pieces; and I wanted to have my Israeli dance club perform and invite everyone to join in. I thought we'd serve kugel, gefilte fish, and Sephardic foods, not beef Wellington. I dreaded getting to the party part and went to great lengths to discourage my friends from attending. My parents kept asking, "Why do you have so few friends coming?" But we don't have the kind of relationship where I could really tell [my mother], and besides, she was having so much fun planning the party she'd always wanted to throw—how could I burst her bubble?

Everet

Empowerment, you say? That was not my experience at all. The caterer called the shots except for when the photographer did. For an hour before my B-Mitzvah, it was standing tall between rotating sets of relatives for photographs. That's a way to prepare inside oneself for leading a service? The photographer stood right over me clicking away when I was reading Torah. He broke up the synergy of people meeting each other to make them pose. Then the DJ called me out of a teary and important discussion with my grandmother to come up to light some candies, and my dad yelled at me for not reading perfectly the lines about family he'd written out for me. The whole scene is too painful to really recall much further. I wish with all my heart we could do it over again.

Sam

My *Bar Mitzvah* became an excuse to hold a referral party for my dad's business associates. I hated every minute of it. I had such a rush of relief and pride when the Torah rituals were over, and a party with real friends and family who care about me would have been just perfect. Why couldn't he hold a referral party full of his medical colleagues at some other time and not have conflated it with my *Bar Mitzvah*! I'm almost thirty and can still feel the disappointment of watching him and Mom work the room, currying favor with those who referred to him. After the ten minutes of family hype from the bandleader, my friends and I went out in back of the catering hall and got high for the first time with some grass from an older cousin. But inside I felt irrelevant, forgotten, and sad. No one ever did come to look for us.

Enough said. These are tender times for feelings, and wounds received at such a crucial time in one's life can linger if we do not address them. In Yiddish we have a saying for such wounds; it is like a small furry familiar animal has suddenly sunk sharp teeth right into your heart. The term for this is creating a *furrible* (some pronounce it fah-raible), and one is born whenever one person so irritates or traumatizes another that their relationship is damaged and even other people sense the toxicity of the energy between you. The weeks and months leading up to life-cycle events are notorious for their high potential for furribles. Tread tenderly, listen deeply, respond generously. And try to forgive off-base things others say during such a time of stress. You are at an advantage already by following the BMAP process, which makes it far less likely you and your team will create these kinds of hurtful scenarios.

Intellectual Expansion

Sara's list of intellectual goals included "exploring the ways young women lived in biblical times, showing how participation in Jewish religious life is changing for those of my gender, and teaching about the situation of women today." She and Ben listed goals relating to finding places where commentators differ on the meaning of a word or verse. Sara declared her intent in this as "to show our guests there have always been many ways to understand the Torah."

During this brainstorming session, their only living grandmother was visiting and the family invited her to participate. The time worked well so Sara's tutor, Joyce, a local rabbinical student, was able to be present as well. Both proved quite helpful in pointing out intriguing possibilities to support her clearly articulated goals.

Sara might want to pay attention to the life of Leah and Jacob's daughter Dinah. This young woman engaged in bold, interesting, and controversial acts from which Sara might learn much about biblical times.

When their grandmother notes that Ben and Sara's paternal grandfather was from Berlin, Germany, the tutor explains that before the war Berlin was a center of Jewish intellectual creativity, including the idea of having one's home serve as a salon for gathering interesting and talented people for fun and an exchange of ideas. Perhaps at Ben and Sara's party the atmosphere of the salon or cabaret of this period could be recreated in some way.

Ben and Sara's maternal great-grandparents were Sephardic Jews. Could this B-Mitzvah have a theme of East meets West and reflect the foods, ideas, music, and contributions of these two very different styles of Jewish culture reflected in their family's history? Grandma specifically suggests inviting someone to paint the hands of Sara and Ben's friends with *hamsas* (symbols of good fortune) and other traditional Jewish and shared Middle Eastern symbols with henna dye at the party. Here is a creative way to add atmosphere, expand the fun, and teach about a fascinating element of Sephardic culture.

The rabbi noted Sara's interest in the life of young women and a desire to show how to interpret Torah from different perspectives, so he pointed to Genesis 31:17. Here, together with their husband, Jacob, Rachel and Leah secretly leave their father Laban's home and set out on a journey to establish a household of their own. When their father catches up with them, he is specifically looking for a missing item known as the *teraphim*. This term appears in Torah only twice: here and in a story about King David. So what can *teraphim* mean? The rabbi offers to help Sara review the commentators' thoughts. Now it happens that Rachel hides the *teraphim* beneath her. The Torah describes her action as "*b'derech nashim*," in "the way of women." What are these mystery terms—*teraphim* and *b'derech nashim*? And what do these stories reveal about the "way of women"? The rabbi has found two excellent Torah sparks to challenge Sara's intellect and imagination.

Upon hearing about the *teraphim*, Ben suggests adding a mystery night for the B-Mitzvah party. A professional storyteller could relate the tale, or the family could stage an interactive play to involve the guests in a search for the mysterious *teraphim*.

Ultimately the family did not adopt these latter two ideas, feeling them too over the top for their friends and family system. Still, when the rabbi shared this novel approach with an adult who was preparing her own B-Mitzvah, the fit proved to be just right. Nowhere is it written that what expands the intellect can't also be fun.

Let's look at some of the new elements in this family's process:

• The family is being patient with the brainstorming process. Decisions are not being made about anything yet; because of this, ideas receive the time necessary to bubble up and flow ever more creatively. Although this might feel a bit overwhelming, the family is really only one session away from beginning to make selections from among all the options.

• By remaining initially flexible on the B-Mitzvah date, it is possible to identify a Torah portion of specific interest to the student. Those who find themselves with assigned dates, however, need not be distressed; in Chapter Five you will find tools to help you discover the messages waiting in that portion that were placed there for the student to find, perhaps since the beginning of time.

- The party has emerged as a creative venue for amplifying the themes that have meaning for this family.
- Sara's role as a young leader is being honored as the family takes up her concern to foster family closeness and helps her figure out how to draw attention to issues of gender and justice in Judaism.
- Issues of physical maturation are coming up for discussion.
- Although Ben might create and sing a ballad as his form of teaching Torah, Sara might elect interpretive dance as her modality. The family is making lots of room to draw upon the students' individual strengths and interests.
- The presence of a grandparent at the planning session revealed the family's Sephardic background, which had almost been overlooked. What better time than B-Mitzvah to celebrate the range of cultures within the Jewish people?
- As family members bring their interests, questions, and passions into the B-Mitzvah process, the Torah's stories and concepts are becoming a source of inspiration, excitement, and even mystery.
- The rabbi, cantor, and tutor are able to serve at their best, as a support system for the B-Mitzvah students and family, offering resources and guidance.

Spiritual Connection

It is helpful to ask questions when forming spiritual goals. Ben's list includes the question, "Will I feel the presence of God when I read from the Torah at my *Bar Mitzvah*?" Sara's list has more questions: "Is there a proper blessing for your first kiss? Do I have to learn all the words in services? Is there a way to pray from your heart?" Ben has also included justice as a spiritual goal; he's wondering, "How can humanity learn to wage peace?" Sara has listed: "How can I help impoverished women and girls?" Most everyone also listed in some way that they want to find significant ways to honor the memory of their Grandpa Daniel, who died this year, within their BMAP.

Sara's tutor explains that the traditional prayers are not intended to be the final word in prayer but rather springboards or guides to finding and expressing the prayer of your heart. She could teach about this in tutoring sessions. What a perfect time to get past the translation of prayers and discover how to use them as doorways to meaning, connection, comfort, hope, and energy for living. Chapter Four and Bmitzvah.org offer substantial guidance for finding meaning in services.

Ben and Sara's dad writes that he sees Grandpa Daniel's qualities in each of them and that he'd like to mention this when he comes up with their mom to give the parents' blessing after the Torah reading at the B-Mitzvah service. To allow yourself and others to invite the memory of a loved one in this way is, in itself, a mitzvah. This idea affects the spirit of those present in a significant way.

Sara has brought an item from the local Jewish newspaper to the session. It describes a United Jewish Communities study that documents single parents' inability to afford to send their children to Jewish summer camp. It is a catch-22: the parent needs to work; the children need sunshine and play. What about Ben and Sara spearheading a family B-Mitzvah project to fund a camp scholarship for such a youth and dedicating it in Grandpa Daniel's name? To affect the spirit and quality of life of another through financial generosity, *tzedakah*, and in doing so to bring honor to the memory of a loved one is a graphic expression of that person's spirituality.

Sara's mother did not have a *Bat Mitzvah*. As a girl she had dearly wanted to do so, but it was forbidden for a woman's voice to be heard from the pulpit in the congregation where she was raised. She would like to talk about her feelings about this when she comes up to give the parents' blessing after Sara reads and interprets the Torah. Raising awareness is an essential component of spiritual practice; awareness can lead to action.

Sara's grandmother imagines Sara inviting those in the room who, like herself and Sara's mother, were not allowed to read from the Torah scroll or, perhaps for other reasons were discouraged from having a *Bar* or *Bat Mitzvah*, to rise in their seats and to then join in blessing Sara and Ben upon achieving B-Mitzvah. This fulfills Sara's intellectual goal of pointing to changes in the empowerment of her gender in our times, and it adds the element of spiritual connection through the generations by physically having those affected rise and empowering them to share in giving a blessing. For Sara's family the process of designing this blessing might become a memorable part of their process. Perhaps they might remember not to take for granted a woman's right to chant and interpret Torah before the community, or to trust that every person's perspective on Torah is important to the development of our people.

Ben added an important dimension to his mother and Sara's concerns about gender and Judaism:

> I would like to call up to the Torah for a blessing all the men in the room who have had a strong influence upon shaping my idea of what it is to live as a Jewish man today. Traditional Judaism emphasized that the role of the woman was to care for the children and the home, and that has changed. Today men are not always at work, at war, or engrossed in study; they are also spending time raising and guiding the youth. I would like to give them a blessing for taking the time to be with us.

Ben has grasped the power of both balance and blessing. Imagine how such words will affect the atmosphere of this B-Mitzvah.

Again this family met with the rabbi and cantor to review the list and their process. When the rabbi heard Ben voice a desire to experience the presence of God, he began to teach him about Reb Nachman of Breslov's belief in the importance of spending time offering the prayer of your heart while outdoors in nature. This type of potentially spiritual experience is very different from reading or talking about God.

The cantor said she could provide Sara with a list of blessings for many occasions and encouraged her to compose a blessing for a first kiss. She also recommended the prayer book *The Book of Blessings* by Rabbi Marcia Falk, which includes thoughts on the formulation of new blessings, and also recommended that the family read *The Path of Blessing* by Rabbi Marcia Prager. Judaism emphasizes the practice of blessing an action or experience with focused attention, for example, eating, putting on new clothes, witnessing a bolt of lightning, and so on. Discovering the benefit of blessing practice is indeed a spiritual goal that helps one to stay awake and filled with wonder and awe for living. Such a practice provides a great lift for the human spirit and is an important life skill.

The tutor also recalled that the life of Dinah has become very interesting to contemporary commentators who commend her desire to "go out and see the daughters of the land" (Genesis 34:1), whereas earlier teachers saw this as acute misbehavior and folly and believed her to have been raped by the very man she wished to marry. Looking at this verse can help Sara and Ben in the intellectual goal of showing their guests how very differently interpreters will relate to a verse's meaning. This verse also reminded the family that Ben's cracking voice is only one of the ways in which he is changing physically. And Sara has asked how to bless a first kiss. B-Mitzvah students are rapidly maturing and statistically proven to be likely to have intimate experiences at ages far, far younger than their parents. The study of such a Torah portion offers an opening for dialogue about seeing sexuality and one's body as a place of lived holiness. This time of initiation is also one for carefully selecting mentors with whom our children can speak openly about matters of gender, physical safety, and independence.

Now the family's process has deepened and expanded, and they are quite excited about the possibilities they are generating.

- Sara and Ben can voice their concerns for social change and begin to give them a practical form. The family is becoming passionate about potential mitzvah projects.
- Those whom the family misses so dearly are going to be remembered in a number of traditional and creative ways during the B-Mitzvah.
- Note that giving room and strategic support to emotional and intellectual concerns and interests has let a new wave of curiosity and opportunity come through about spiritual experience. Had the family dismissed Ben's sharing of his anxiety about public speaking, the safety and respect needed during this process and among team members for discussion about other personal issues would have been damaged or lost.

- Prayer and reading from the Torah are no longer viewed as arduous rites of task memorization; they are serving as resources for healing, connection, and personal growth.
- The rapid physical changes adolescent B-Mitzvah students are undergoing can be recognized in a context of holiness that allows for healthy discussion and mentoring.
- This family is empowered and guided in ways that create meaningful involvement for everyone involved in the B-Mitzvah. Judaism is opening up for them as a spiritual path.

Logistical Excellence

Bringing ones hopes and dreams into the world of physicality and action means going through each chosen objective and deciding what its successful implementation will require. This is the realm of who, how, where, when, and what.

Now the B-Mitzvah student goes back through the planning documents to highlight each strategy he hopes to implement. Someone from the planning team should help with this step.

At the next planning session, the student presents the items she has highlighted for implementation. If the student has not chosen a team member's hoped-for items, it is fine for the team member to raise that item for discussion to see if the student will be amenable or appreciative if someone else implements the point. It is not fair to force an issue. Keep in mind that wanting to "win" on any given point can easily damage the spirit of the event and the student. Winning is not the goal; the goal is growing in all four dimensions to the extent the student is available to do so. And if there are difficult consequences to be experienced regarding a decision, that too affords healthy learning opportunities for all involved.

By taking the points the team has agreed on and formulating those into a paragraph for each dimension, you will soon have your BMAP mission statement. The entire team can help to pull this statement together. Here's how Ben and Sara's looked at this stage of the process:

Ben and Sara's BMAP Mission Statement

Emotional: We want our B-Mitzvah to reflect our individual interests and talents. We expect to work hard and have great accomplishments during this process and to experience our family's pride in us for what we will have experienced and learned and how we go about sharing this with those who attend the B-Mitzvah ceremony and celebration.

We also want our guests to feel honored, to have a pleasurable and meaningful time, and we will use our artistic abilities in dance and music to help our guests feel connected to the Torah and services. Ben will write a ballad about the twins Jacob and Esau. He plans for our guests to join in singing the refrain. Sara intends to create a dance to reveal what she discovers while studying about Leah and her daughter Dina.

Intellectual: We have found a theme for our studies and the B-Mitzvah day: difference. Ben wants to focus on differences between the twins Jacob and Esau; Sara is concerned about gender and Judaism. One way in which our own Jewish family heritage is different is that we have a grandparent from Morocco. We want to research this part of our heritage and incorporate Sephardic music, dance, art, and foods into our service and party along with Eastern European traditions.

Spiritual: We would very much like to go beyond all the memorization in order to experience a connection to God when we pray and read Torah, and through sharing Shabbat and celebration. We are curious about the idea of learning about blessings, inventing some of our own, and blessing the new roles of Jewish men and women as part of our service. We will also work for justice by establishing a summer camp scholarship for children of single parents and dedicating it in memory of Grandpa Daniel. We hope by learning how to do a *Havdalah* ceremony and offering this as guests arrive for the party, we can honor the differences of all who attend and create a holiness and happiness that flows from Shabbat into our celebration.

Appropriately, the plan is simplified and has harmonized many of the ideas that came out during the planning process. The plan is rich in culture, learning, creativity, and fun. The students and family are proud of and excited by their plan and ready to move on to the phase of sorting out logistics.

Translating Strategy Into Reality

Now this family is ready to get down to details of budget, location, suppliers, helpers, and timing. Basic choices will be heavily influenced by their planning process; the theme of difference and incorporation of a Sephardic influence will inspire the selection of invitations, musicians, ritual items, Ben's tutor, and decorations.

Ben would like a tutor who can also guide his musical abilities, so he decides to put notes up at the local music schools, area colleges, and community centers, seeking someone who has a good combination of Jewish skills and musical interests to work with him.

Sara wants her *tallit* (prayer shawl) to be decorated with designs of the type her grandmother spoke about as part of Jewish culture in Morocco. Using the *tallit* how-to diagram at Bmitzvah.org she hopes to make her own with help from a teacher at school, or just maybe someone in the extended family will support her to commission a Jewish fabric artist to undertake her idea.

Ben and Sara want their invitation to reflect the theme of distinctions and also their respective favorite colors of blue and green. They will visit an engraving and party business nearby with their mom to learn about what's involved in developing invitations, not just color and content, but timing.

Their mom works all day as an attorney, and their dad is an author who works from home. After a big discussion about the budget and whether to research Jewish ethnic foods and make and freeze them for a self-catered party, everyone agrees on the idea of a Middle Eastern buffet. Their dad will research options to make this possible and report back at the next family meeting.

Notice how the BMAP process has resulted in parents who are team players rather than taskmasters. A helpful analogy might be that of a race car driver. The B-Mitzvah student is the driver. The driver needs a talented, carefully coordinated technical support team. On this team are trainers of many sorts whom the driver consults for help with honing skills and instincts, designing tools and garments, doing advance promotion, providing emotional support, and organizing a celebration. God willing, everyone will cross the finish line of becoming age thirteen and will be regarded as a Jewish adult; the quality of the B-Mitzvah journey becomes very different when a family follows the BMAP process.

In order to provide you with a broad vision of the exciting range of learning and ritual possibilities for B-Mitzvah, this chapter used as an example a family that is knowledgeable about tradition and religious practice. Many people are fairly rusty at their Judaism or find themselves newly attracted to Jewish spirituality. The BMAP has lots of room for the needs and abilities of every kind of student and family to manifest. And upcoming chapters will provide lots of details about the nature of Jewish tradition and practice. Meanwhile, underneath all of the creativity is a fairly simple model because the BMAP team is designing three major processes:

1. A period of preparation for the B-Mitzvah student
2. A culminating ritual during services, up at the Torah, which demonstrates the effect of the students preparation before the community's eyes and marks this rite of passage with formal recognition and blessing
3. A celebration with family and friends for having achieved this rite of passage

The student's mission is fourfold:

1. To know how to participate in the core religious practices of the Jewish people
2. To be increasingly self-aware of talents, traits, and the influence of personal and collective history upon one's feelings, thoughts, and actions; to develop, express, and reveal oneself through this process
3. To be able to identify the need for change and healing in the world and to make a mitzvah by experimenting with taking a role in making some change and healing happen

4. To undertake a major challenge, to be able to read aloud from the Jewish people's most sacred text, the Torah, in the sacred language, Hebrew, and to interpret that reading in a way that will help those present experience meaning for living

To achieve the mission, the student needs a supportive team and community. The team should consist first of an inner circle of those who will help with logistics, planning, and creativity. Instructor(s) and mentor(s), perhaps those with special, related interests and skills with whom to consult, form the next circle. Guests who are connected to and care about the student surround them. Finally, the student needs a community, whether an existing one or a group called into existence to help with this process, those with whom the student will live Judaism as a system of sacred practices that offer meaning and support for living.

A planning process makes for satisfaction and excellence in carrying out the student's mission. The process should include the following elements:

- Selection of a regular meeting time for the B-Mitzvah team
- Formulation of emotional, intellectual, and spiritual goals
- Translation of the goals into desirable objectives
- Selection of satisfying objectives in each category
- Creation of a mission statement from the objectives
- Review of the objectives with an eye to what logistics are needed
- Details on who agrees to be responsible for which items in the plan and by when

It's time to plunge in, to begin by having the student enter a process of self-assessment. What skills, talents, interests, life history, and learning style does the student bring to this adventure? These will be important clues for designing an effective and exciting journey of preparation.

Chapter Three

Incorporating Awareness, Talents & Interests

This season of life offers a concentrated opportunity to expand the way you look at your world, your Judaism, and yourself. As a rite of initiation, *Bar/Bat Mitzvah* (B-Mitzvah) preparation begins with knowing yourself as someone who is evolving—who can make choices, learn from life experiences, teach others, and formulate important questions for exploration.

If you are an adult choosing to undertake B-Mitzvah studies, this process offers the rare opportunity to take charge of your own learning, select your teachers, decide what studies will have the significance and balance to lend integrity to your process, and celebrate your qualities of being and the story of your life. For many of today's adults and parents, the great beauty within Judaism was obscured by the inadequate nature of their post-Holocaust Hebrew school education and the rote or limited practice of Judaism at home. So going back for B-Mitzvah studies can also be a season of healing and rededication for you and your Judaism.

For a youth undertaking B-Mitzvah, this marks the beginning of your right to have greater power and influence within your family. In childhood you looked to your parents and other adults to teach you the norms of the world—how to behave and what to know. Now you are beginning a process of collaborating with them in shaping your world and the world of the future. Ultimately, parents still have responsibility for your safety and support for a few more years, but within these parameters are broad options for taking responsibility and leading an exciting, fulfilling, conscious life.

Testing limits and boundaries is common for a young adult. Some choose the road of acting out through having sex, smoking, or drinking. There's another way to stretch yourself and those around you—use your power to expand who you are and who you want to become. Know yourself, and then make a plan for what more you need to know and be able to do.

Knowing yourself is a many-faceted, lifelong project. Let's begin with the type of knowledge that bears directly on your success in this great adventure of creating a meaningful B-Mitzvah—identifying your learning style.

Know Your Style Of Learning

Everyone brings something incredibly unique to the gifts and challenges called life. We all bring the individual self. The self is notable for our talents and personality, as well as intellectual and physical strengths and limitations.

For example, you might love the color turquoise and dislike olive green, tend to be quick to answer a question and yet patient during a biology experiment, shy at school and surprisingly outgoing with elders, talented at sports and musically tone deaf, or precisely the opposite or any shade in between.

The process of preparing for a B-Mitzvah becomes easier when the people involved know themselves: personality, talents, learning styles, preferences, and interests. It's possible to identify your learning style, for example.

The Jewish people's term for education is learning, not studying. It's possible to study copiously in a style that gets you nowhere slowly—that's not learning! This season of your life is a great time to seek out those who can teach via your best learning style.

The ideas you are about to read in this chapter, although commonly accepted to be true, are not sufficiently implemented within public and Jewish educational settings. So many of us are frustrated, shamed, or blocked in our learning because teachers are not trained to respect and respond to different learning styles. Show this section to your teachers in a loving way. They are likely to be excited and interested to follow up in their own training. Teachers also get sad and frustrated when their students can't learn.

Researcher Howard Gardner has identified nine learning styles, which he calls multiple intelligences: Verbal, Visual, Kinesthetic (touch/movement), Musical, Logical, Naturalist (outdoors/nature), Interpersonal, Intrapersonal, Existential (need big picture). The Styles of Learning exercise that follows, which includes three basic styles, can help you discover what your general learning style is. If you often feel frustrated in your ability to learn, you may want to seek out a professional who can take you through a more comprehensive learning analysis and create a customized program to help you discover your best learning methods and hidden learning talents.

What do the totals tell you about your learning strengths? Is your highest number in one category, or do your scores reveal that you have a mixture of strengths? Here is a basic guide to working with your results.

If you are an auditory learner, you may be someone who easily memorizes the verses of popular music. This is a clue to tape sessions with your teachers and tutors for repeated listening. Take notes and review them frequently; write a summary and then say or sing it out loud. Talk back to facts, figures, characters, and symbols in your studies; listen for their voices and ideas. Take what you have just learned and retell it to someone else; it will remain with you much longer.

If you are a visual learner, seek out and create charts, maps, flash cards, or even animations that you can watch morph on your computer screen. Visualize or picture words and concepts in your head. Be playful; set ideas into images that you can recall because of their location in the image. Read and reread; let yourself notice new words and ideas each time. You don't have to catch everything on the first round.

If you are a kinesthetic learner, you may normally jingle something in your pocket while listening to someone, or you may find yourself doodling, knitting, or stacking potato chips— actions others might

DISCOVERING YOUR LEARNING STRENGTHS			
Description of Learning Style	Auditory	Visual	Kinesthetic
I follow oral instructions better than written ones.	■		
When I'm interested in a topic, I'll read up on it in depth.		■	
I'm good at jigsaw puzzles and mazes.		■	
Best way to remember things? By picturing them in my head.		■	
I recall more of what I hear than of what I read.	■		
I learn through my fingers; it's important for me to type or write something down myself.			■
I prefer projects where I can learn or teach about something by making a model of it or creating some other visual interpretation of it.			■
If I set something to music, even a mathematical formula, I can remember it more easily.	■		
If I spell or read out loud, I remember material better.	■		

DISCOVERING YOUR LEARNING STRENGTHS			
Description of Learning Style	Auditory	Visual	Kinesthetic
I'm better able to focus if I have something to unconsciously fidget with—coins, an eraser, keys, and so on.			
Chewing gum or snacking helps me focus.			
When visual aids are present (such as tables and charts, movies, slides), I am better able to learn.			
Total			

interpret as your being distracted, but you know these actions really help you to focus. Kinesthetic learners often find it helpful to write out what they want to learn several times. Try to dance, act, sing, or compose into music what you are trying to learn or develop. Paint or sculpt your ideas and feelings about the material you are working on learning. You might pull up a drum or a desktop and support your lesson by turning it into a chant or a rhythm.

It makes all the difference in the world to be able to enjoy learning as you are naturally inclined. Few will fit exactly into the categories in the exercise, so consider them guides, not rigid rules. Your enthusiastic support of your teachers' efforts to embrace these ideas might help generations of students who follow you. That too is a mitzvah!

Know Your Talents And Skills

B-Mitzvah is a time to let your talents shine. All of your talents and skills will likely be relevant to this phase of your life in some way. On the day of the B-Mitzvah, the guests are coming to experience Shabbat, Torah, family, and celebration through the lens of who the student is. So because B-Mitzvah includes a substantial period of being in training, it is a good time to do a self-assessment like the one above.

The information you glean will help with setting up goals and challenges for yourself so that you will stretch toward your potential in some areas and best use your superior talents in others.

Know Your Personality

However you might describe yourself today, most likely you are changing quickly. Preferences for food, music, entertainment, and lots more change over the years. Your environment, a move to a new neighborhood, a change of schools, changes in the family, new siblings, divorces, remarriages, illness—life's traumas and treats change a person. On the journey some of us discover hidden talents or the need for new or improved skills; all along the way physical changes are taking hold, sometimes in abundance.

Also changing is one's personality. The word personality comes from the term persona, which is from the Latin, personarare, "to sound through." In ancient Greek and Roman theater, each actor wore a mask (called a persona) to help convey the actor's role to the audience and to amplify the voice. So B-Mitzvah, like theater, isn't just where you recite the words in the script of tradition, it is where who you are makes the day particularly special. Stepping up to the plate as a reader and teacher of Torah at B-Mitzvah is a moment when your newest persona is visible. Your persona at any point in your life is a combination of who you really are, what society expects you to be, and who you are becoming.

APPRECIATING YOUR TALENTS AND SKILLS

Check one column (Strong, Mild, or I Need or Want to Grow in This) for each of the talents in this exercise and fill in an idea for how to apply this talent to your B-Mitzvah. Follow the example given at "Sports." Feel free to add additional categories of talents.

B-Mitzvah Student's Talent	Strong	Mild	Not Very Developed Yet	I Need or Want to Grow in This	Idea for How to Apply This Talent to My B-Mitzvah
Sports; baseball, football, track, volleyball, swimming, other	X				I play baseball. The metaphors from this sport could become part of my *d'var Torah*. I could talk about how being up at the Torah is "being in the zone" with God and of Joseph's interpretation of Pharaoh's dream as a home run.
Shopping					
Making and following a budget					
Vocal quality					
Noticing details					
Helping people feel welcome					
Expressive dance or movement					
Discipline and focus					(Continued)

B-Mitzvah Student's Talent	Strong	Mild	Not Very Developed Yet	I Need or Want to Grow in This	Idea for How to Apply This Talent to My B-Mitzvah
Writing music					
Cooking					
Ability to learn languages					
Ability to teach an idea, concept, or skill to others					
Organizing					
Handling conflict					
Expressing my feelings					
Comforting					
Visual arts: painting, weaving, sculpture, drawing, photography, other					
Listening					
Following current events					
Martial arts					
Staying on schedule					
Receiving feedback					

B-Mitzvah Student's Talent	Strong	Mild	Not Very Developed Yet	I Need or Want to Grow in This	Idea for How to Apply This Talent to My B-Mitzvah
Playing instrument(s)					
Critiquing					
Public speaking					
Singing					
Learning through reading					
Making websites					
Sense of humor					
Love to be out in or sudy nature					
Add More Talents:					

Here are some basic principles to consider when evaluating your own personality.

Your persona is intended to protect you. You radiate a persona with the intent to attract those you desire to have near and to deflect those with whom you prefer not to have contact.

Your persona takes on added power in certain settings. For example, this might happen if you become head of student council or editor of a student newspaper or when you acquire the authority of the pulpit at your B-Mitzvah.

Your persona changes. You might meet a very warm, welcoming person and want to emulate her. When you do, you will succeed at bringing out a part of yourself that might not have been activated before.

Take out a notebook to serve as a your B-Mitzvah journal and think of a few people whom you admire. Pick one and write out a description of his or her persona. Following are two sample descriptions:

Youth Example

My new best friend Elliot always invites new kids along to play soccer at camp. I was afraid of him when we were younger because he had a bad temper and would kick the ball right into me deliberately and it hurt. He changed about two years ago and stopped being an angry person. Now I'd say he's more a curious person. He asks friendly questions and makes the new kids feel welcome. I admire his ability to change and often wonder whether to ask him how he did it.

Adult Example

My friend Ellen is so attentive to guests. She notices if a desk is too high for comfortable computing or if the room needs more lighting. She tries new things to expand her abilities as a therapist and after all these years still elects to pay someone to review her cases each month. I admire her integrity. Also she has clear boundaries professionally and personally; she lets house guests know how long they are invited for and which rooms are available for exploration. The walls of her home are like a canvas for her self-expression—

pictures of ancestors, friends, collected pieces from many cultures, and paintings of sweet moments of spirit between people adorn her walls. I greatly admire her creativity, integrity, and sensitivity to those around her.

Now explore the following two questions, using your own learning styles, and then note your findings in your journal.

Many who come to your B-Mitzvah will not have seen you in quite some time. How would you describe major changes in your persona over the years?

If an overseas pen pal asked for a description of what you are like as a person, what would be your most true self-description?

Know The Story Of Your Life

Judaism places tremendous importance on the story of a person's life. Close to the end of the Torah, in the *parsha* known as *Ekev* in the book of *Devarim*, Deuteronomy, Moses tells the people to "Remember the whole journey," because it is "not by bread alone that a person lives." By reflecting upon your life's journey thus far, you can uncover lots of helpful ideas for everything from deciding where to hold your B-Mitzvah to what you want to emphasize in your *d'var Torah*, studies, and celebration.

Feelings aren't right or wrong; they are just how you truly remember your life. If you decide to share some of your responses with your B-Mitzvah support team, a mentor, or family member(s), let them know that during such sharing people need to be careful not to try to correct other people's perceptions. Your feelings are your feelings. People often remember things differently; that's OK. Try to see the sharing as interesting data and not grounds for debate or damage.

Some of what you realize in this process might arouse strong memories and feelings. This is vital information for you to work with in your life. You, by definition, can't be objective about yourself. Help actually helps. Moses was always climbing a mountain to speak with

Tradition

Becoming What You Are Becoming
The capacity to grow and change is one of the ways that Judaism considers humans to have been made in the image of God, *b'tzelem Elohim*. This idea has a beautiful source in the Torah, Genesis 1:28.

> During one of Moses' early desert adventures, he hears a message coming into his consciousness while he stands before a very odd bush that is on fire yet doesn't get used up or ever burned out.
>
> Bemused, Moses asks: "With whom can I say I have been speaking?"
>
> The answer that comes back to him is not a regular name like Amenhotep, Harry, Sylvia, or God. The answer is: *"Ehyeh imach"* or "I Will Be is with you."
>
> Huh? What kind of name is that? When he asks a second time, again the answer comes: *"Ehyeh asher Ehyeh"* or "I Will Be What I Will Be."

Wow. That's quite a way to want to be identified, as pure change. The Hebrew can also be translated as "I Am Becoming What I Am Becoming."

Who alive couldn't say that? "I am Becoming What I Am Becoming." Everyone and everything is constantly aging, evolving, learning, changing. You are indeed, *b'tzelem Elohim*, created in the image of God. You can't be pinned down with labels, because you, too, are blessed with the capacity for and the inevitability of changing.

RECORDING THE STORY OF YOUR LIFE

Take the questions that follow slowly, working on them in your journal or contemplating them one at a time, perhaps before bed. You might create a B-Mitzvah-year diary and begin it by copying these questions into it and leaving room for your answers. It might be helpful to have photo albums close at hand as a research tool during this exercise.

Although it's fine to invite family, teachers, and friends into this process, for most youth, B-Mitzvah is a season when the need for privacy increases. For adult B-Mitzvah students, it is often the opposite, where the process of discovery within the family is enhanced by openness. In either case, you don't have to share any of your answers. If sharing brings you insight and joy, do so. If not, hold back on all or some of your diary entries. You have the power over information about yourself. Your answers are your own business!

May you be blessed to have this way of reflecting on your life serve you as a precious source of personal enrichment.

Where do you live now? Where have you lived? (Include the country, state, neighborhood, and kind of dwelling.)

List any pets you have had over the years. Were some favorites? How has your relationship with your pets changed, that is, do you take more or less responsibility for them? If you haven't had pets and have feelings about this, you might want to write about that. Do you see having a pet in your future?

What activities (art, sports, reading, music, computer, and so on) did and do you like to do? What did you have to do? Did you have a favorite instructor or a favorite experience? Who or what? Why?

Do you collect anything? Has what you collect changed over time?

RECORDING THE STORY OF YOUR LIFE

List favorite songs and musicians for as far back as you can remember in your life.

Every person is a unique work of art; appearance changes so much as one grows up. How was your hair styled in the past (check out your photo albums) and now?

What kind of clothes do you like to wear? How has this changed over the years?

Did you have an imaginary friend as a child? A special blanket or must-hold toy? Is there something that gives you comfort now?

Did or do you go to Hebrew school or religious school? Describe a few of your favorite and least favorite teachers, subjects, and experiences.

Looking back, what were some important playthings of yours? What are your playthings now?

What were your friends like in the past? What are they like now?

RECORDING THE STORY OF YOUR LIFE

Who are some problem people in your life now? Who have some problem people been before?

Who is and has been most involved in raising you? How is this for you?

Consider how you remember your relationship with parent(s) or guardian(s) changing over time.

Recall secret or private spots you have and have had for hiding in or hanging out.

What about physical changes—height, hair style, taking on a more womanly or manly body and emotions? How are you feeling about the pace and effect of these changes?

Where did you go to school? How did you feel about it? Which teachers did you like and which not and why? What about favorite subjects and memorable projects?

Do you have a favorite color? Have your favorite things, colors, foods, and experiences changed over the years?

RECORDING THE STORY OF YOUR LIFE

Did anyone special enter your family life during this time? Do you have siblings, stepparents, or stepsiblings? How is your relationship evolving with them?

Name your biggest fears.

Looking back, what events, trips, or experiences have made an impact on you?

Have you ever had crushes or the experience of being happily or unhappily in love?

Moses longed to get to the Promised Land. What are your longings?

Has anything ever happened to you that seemed like an unexpected gift or challenge from God?

Questions of your own:

the Head Consultant. The strong and wise seek advisers; as part of becoming strong and wise, you can seek out mentors and professional advisers like therapists, too.

Keep your exercise, Recording the Story of Your Life, in a safe place. As this year unfolds, you may want to review and reflect further on it. Imagine if your mom or grandfather had such a journal tucked away from when she or he was your age, wouldn't that be something to read! So hold yours close; the torah of your own life is also a treasure.

Let's look at a few examples of how other students have responded to some of the Story of Your Life questions.

Ken

While completing the section about the places he's lived, B-Mitzvah student Ken realized that housing issues had greatly affected his life's story. Most of his childhood, he lived in tight quarters with three siblings in an apartment. Now that he was becoming a teen, Ken yearned for the privacy of a room of his own, so he was both excited and anxious for construction on a family house to be completed.

Ken's Torah portion included the mitzvah of sitting in a *sukkah*. A *sukkah* is an easy-to-build structure reminiscent of harvest huts from biblical times. It is traditional to eat meals outside in nature within the sukkah for one whole week each year during the holiday called *Sukkot* (*Sukkos*). Ken had never experienced a *sukkah*, so with the agreement of the builder and his family, he designated one of his B-Mitzvah learning goals as building a *sukkah* outside their new home and experiencing its practices. He even slept in there under the stars one night.

Ken's tutor pointed out that Shelter is one of the names for God in the Torah. Ken's wondering about that led him to choose a mitzvah project involving volunteer work at a local shelter for homeless people. After a while he wanted to help even more and so included a request for donations to both the local shelter and a shelter for abused women in Israel in his B-Mitzvah invitation.

- Ken's exploration of his responses to Know the Story of Your Life opened up a connection between his Torah portion and his life.

- A mitzvah and its associated holiday opened up for him as an organic, exciting, and empowering choice.
- Ken made a powerful theological statement by becoming the hands of God through his work at the homeless shelter.
- He concerned himself with both the local community and the needs of his people in Israel in the design of his mitzvah work.
- Ultimately, his *d'var Torah* was very rich because of the synergy of these experiences.
- A little-known uncle who was handy with tools got involved with him in the sukkah construction project and became an important part of Ken's teenage years.

Sandra

Sandra's creativity was triggered by the question about pets. She has always had pets and feels tremendous compassion for animals.

Sandra's Torah portion was all about the sacrificial system. At first she became horrified by what she read, and then she realized with pride that Judaism has evolved tremendously.

She decided to collect *midrash* (Jewish stories that comment on Torah) on the subject of having compassion for animals and to sprinkle them as inspirational readings through a booklet she and her parents made to hold creative readings for her B-Mitzvah service.

During an on-line search for *midrash*, Sandra discovered the Coalition on the Environment and Jewish Life (COEJL). For her mitzvah project, she got almost her whole class to take out memberships in COEJL, and she organized her family to sponsor a COEJL speaker for a school assembly.

- Sandra discovered the secret to Judaism's longevity: it is an evolving system.
- She became a teacher of Torah by inspiring others to the mitzvah known as *tzaar baalei chayyim*, the prevention of unnecessary pain to animals. She did this through her use of *midrashim* in her B-Mitzvah service.
- She became a Jewish activist by joining COEJL, organizing the environmentalism lecture, and engaging her peers in joining the organization.

Andi

When Andi looked at her answers to the Recording the Story of Your Life questions, she realized how very much her parents' divorce and her mother's remarriage, which gave her both a stepfather and two stepbrothers, had affected her life.

Andi decided her recombined family experience has something in common with the Exodus story in her Torah portion. Those who left Egypt had to learn how to get along in the wilderness together, and that way an amazing new nation was born.

Her greatest fear had been that her mom would remarry and, after developing a comfortable new life, it would all change radically again. Looking back, she realized how much she has come to appreciate her new family situation and that she has some wisdom to offer about such changes.

Andi decided to give her *d'var Torah* on this idea of overcoming fear of change and learning how to adapt to new conditions.

For an individual *aliyah*, the honor of coming up to the *bimah* (stage) to witness the Torah reading, she called up each member of her two families: her dad and his girlfriend, her mom and stepdad, her two older stepsiblings, and her grandparents. As each came up, she shared a little moment from the process of getting to know them and gave them each a blessing. And she also shared how she'd come to see new sides of her dad as he also adapted to the changes. After the Torah reading, Andi invited everyone in the room who wanted a blessing for finding meaning and value inside of feared changes to rise. She then sang a short blessing for changes that she had composed with her rabbi's help.

- Andi discovered how the Torah offers meaning for living.
- In reviewing her life, she learned how to draw strength from change and to realize she has already developed some life wisdom.
- She honored her family in a personal, equal, and thoughtful way.
- Andi embraced everyone present by finding a universal theme and used her moment of pulpit power to honor the human fear of change and find within it a source of blessing.

Dana

Dana is deeply into art, color, and texture. His Recording the Story of Your Life responses include a long list of changes in his favorite colors over the years.

Dana's interest in color proved to be a happy coincidence because his Torah portion frequently mentions both fabrics and colors. The portion is about building sacred space, the *mishkan*, the portable sanctuary that the Israelites used in the wilderness. Dana's inspiration from this became to learn whether various colors hold particular significance in Judaism.

He discovered that in Jewish mystical tradition, Kabbalah, each branch of the Tree of Life has a different associated color and qualities that a person can improve in himself. (To learn more about the kabbalists' self-improvement practices, visit ReclaimingJudaism. org.)

Dana decided to create colorful banners to decorate the synagogue that would offer this Tree of Life interpretation, and he also carried the theme into his party and invitations.

Through an on-line search, he found a nearby Jewish artist who made paintings about the Tree of Life, and he studied the colors and qualities with her as part of his B-Mitzvah preparation. She recommended that he also work on the qualities in himself and keep a journal on his progress, which he did, creating a technicolor diary that became a personal treasure.

Dana donated the banners to the temple as his mitzvah project and joyfully explained them as his *d'var Torah*.

- Dana's gift as an artist became his way of discovering Jewish art.
- This led him to search out and find a mentor sensitive to art, youth, and Jewish spiritual practice.
- He learned a powerful practice that some say goes all the way back to the Garden of Eden, how to focus on personal qualities through the *eitz chayyim*, the Tree of Life.
- His congregation was delighted at the quality of his art and thrilled at the donation of the banners.

The Personal Kehillah

The term for community in Hebrew is *kehillah*. Popular culture has put an end to the communal tribal storytelling circle. Youth once learned how to navigate the waters of life by hearing elders' public recounting of how they overcame obstacles and adversity. Too often we discuss life's challenges behind closed doors, such as in a therapist's office. Mentoring in skills for an increasingly adult life needs to be provided for our youth. Also, people wear a variety of hats in life. The ability to discern different roles is part of maturing. A substantial project worth considering is formation of one of many possible types of personal *kehillah*.

A *personal kehillah* is an advisory form of community, a discussion and support group that offers deep listening and guidance. This council can be for the B-Mitzvah student or for the parents. It is composed of respected adults and perhaps a few older teen cousins or neighbors. The *kehillah* meets for about a year at regular intervals with the B-Mitzvah student to share wisdom about how to navigate life, develop shared life stories, and establish caring connections. Ten, a *minyan*, is a good size for *kehillah* membership.

A young student has the right to veto someone's presence on the council, as well as to suggest additions. Parents have the right to veto additions that make them uncomfortable as well. Those forming a parenting *kehillah* are advised to tactfully make sure your *kehillah* members are all willing to serve together.

The *kehillah* might meet first without the student(s) whom the group will be helping to initiate. This is a time to speak about what it means to serve in such a role. How might such a support experience have made a difference to the *kehillah* members in their lives? Strong feelings may come up.

Agree upon a simple ritual structure. Perhaps each session will open with the reading of a poem or chanting of a sacred phrase. A shofar might be placed in the center as the object each person will hold while speaking. Agree to have a timekeeper, so that each person has equal opportunity for sharing. Take turns bringing healthy refreshments.

What will you talk about month after month? A starter suggestion: What roles might a person take on or encounter in life? Examples are:

- Citizen
- Scholar
- Activist
- Journalist
- Scholar
- Law enforcement agent
- Philanthropist
- Parent
- Artist
- Mensch
- Sports enthusiast
- Friend
- Woman, man
- Soldier
- Music lover
- Juror
- Teacher
- Health professional
- Teen
- Sibling

Another discussion sequence a *kehillah* might select would be to address a different life challenge at each gathering, such as the following:

- How to get a new idea of yours taken seriously
- Response options when confronted by an anti-Semitic incident or comment
- How to approach someone to speak about a difficult topic or interpersonal problem
- How to handle anger, grief, fear, or disappointments
- What to do when someone makes an inappropriate physical advance

- How to deal with premenstrual syndrome and other hormonal surges
- How to respond effectively when someone knocks down something you believe in

Bring poetry, visualizations, music, and other resources that shed light on the subject.

The group should establish ground rules for communication. For example, try not to speak abstractly during sessions; draw instead on personal experience. It is very important not to correct anyone at such sessions. Answers to guidance topics are subjective. Everyone must share what is true for them. At all times the B-Mitzvah student has an equal voice in the *kehillah* and an added right—to raise any new question and ask any member of the council for private discussion time or clarification.

Some find it helpful to have these councils be of the same gender as the B-Mitzvah student. There are unique aspects and issues to forming a male or female identity, and cultivating role models and mentors simultaneously for this facet of life is very important.

The month prior to the B-Mitzvah ritual, the *kehillah* might take the student out camping for a Jewish vision quest experience (see Chapter Four) and a blessing ritual in which *kehillah* members describe and honor the student's strengths, struggles, and growth. A custom to use after each person shares is to say, "*Shamati*, I have sh'ma-ed, 'listened,' deeply to the torah of your life."

The final meeting of the personal *kehillah* might be the month following the B-Mitzvah ritual. The B-Mitzvah initiate might conduct this meeting, leading the opening chant or poem. The initiate might take up the shofar or other power object and say: "Now that I have passed my initiation as a Jewish wo/man, let me tell you the highlights of my B-Mitzvah, the glorious as well as the sorry points, for such is the sacred journey called life."

Next, members of the *kehillah* could share their favorite memories from the B-Mitzvah.

The B-Mitzvah initiate could now give each person a gift, specially selected or made to reflect an understanding of who that person truly is, in appreciation for the gift of this person's support and wisdom through the B-Mitzvah process.

Sometimes such a personal *kehillah* might choose to continue, perhaps shifting emphasis and composition to deal with the life of another member of this bonded community. As the idea catches on, members may be needed to serve in new *kehillot*, for other young persons. This approach can also be adapted to serve a small B-Mitzvah class.

Another model to consider is a youth-only council, such as the early teen group program that focuses on life skills—Rosh Chodesh Is for Girls!—and Shevet Achim: The Brotherhood, greatly needed, innovative

Tip

Knowing Your Voice

The ability to create a pleasant musical sound can virtually always be learned. Tone-deafness is curable. We have seen qualified vocal coaches work wonders, not only with those who have musical talent but with those who appear to have none. This is worth pursuing; vocal training can change your life. And learning vocal warm-ups and cool down exercises can save your voice from damage during practice.

There is a Jewish aphorism, "The body is the instrument on which the soul plays life for God." No matter how tone deaf or exceptional a singer you believe yourself to be, it is possible to learn how to enhance your sound. Most of us are unconscious of how many different techniques there are to shape a vocal sound. This is actually fascinating, fun to do, and possible at any age. Even a few sessions are worth it.

How to find a vocal coach? Ask a local cantor or choir director; many cantors maintain a life-long relationship with their vocal coach. Or to find a vocal coach, ask at any local college or seminary music department, or do a keyword search on-line specifying your geographic location plus the phrase *vocal coach*.

programs offered by Moving Traditions that are "appropriate for all varieties of Jewish families." Learn more: Movingtraditions.org

There is even more of interest to be found in the details of a person's life. Looking back, how have you changed? What have been your challenges? What opportunities have mattered most? How have you been shaped by your family's choice of neighbors? What teachers have mattered most? What talents and hobbies are you cultivating for yourself? What do you care about most? What brings you joy?

The torah of *your* life, your story, is an important lens through which you look out at the world. This is part of knowing yourself, contemplating your story so far. Your story is full of clues about how where you've been has shaped who you are. And all of it is an important factor in determining what kind of B-Mitzvah you want to create.

Know Your Own Soul

Along with your talents, personality, and intellectual and physical abilities, Judaism has a unique way to describe a whole additional set of assets placed within every human. These include the capacities to feel, reflect, analyze, learn, innovate, intuit, hope, pray, and change, and to influence the environment, family, and community and be influenced in turn. These remarkable qualities are described in Judaism as dimensions of the soul.

The Jewish mystical tradition considers the essence of your life to be a soul spark from the original burst of energy that resulted in creation as we know it. The dimensions of a candle's flame are another helpful Jewish model for the soul. You may have noticed that candles are important in Judaism— for beginning and ending Shabbat, holy days, Hanukkah, and as a memorial for a soul. This is indeed because the flame is our symbol for the many levels of the human soul.

It is traditional to question spiritual teachings, to see them as possibilities that you can test out. Understanding Your Soul offers an opportunity to see whether you really do have a soul and how to sense it.

UNDERSTANDING YOUR SOUL

Directions: Check off each aspect of the soul listed here that you believe exists in you. Test whether this model offers something useful for the process of getting to know the parts of yourself that have lots of room for expansion. Notice that Judaism has many words for the soul.

Can you feel the difference between each dimension? Try following each of these levels after blessing the Shabbat, holiday, or Hanukkah candles. How does the meaning of the flame change for you?

Note: "ch" is pronounced gutturally as "kh."

Diagram at http://reclaimingjudaism.org/teachings/guided-meditation-flame

Part of the Flame	Symbolizes	Hebrew Term
Wick	Body	*Guf*
Blue core color of flame	Where your soul seems to connect with your body. Where does this seem to be for you?	*Nefesh*
Yellow band of the flame	Your emotions, uniqueness, personality, and potential	*Ruach*
Orange band of the flame	Your ability to think, reason, innovate, remember, and create	*Neshamah*
Black smoky frizzles coming off the flame	The life force that keeps you going and your intuition	*Chayah*
Heat and light	Like a drop in the ocean, where the heat of your life cannot be distinguished from that of all life forms; where your story and the consequences of your effects on others through your ideas, words, and deeds extend beyond you, where all is One	*Yechidah*

This chapter supports awareness of the fascinating inner journey. So much more than flesh and blood, you are a remarkable, evolving being. Judaism is designed to help your soul soar, heal, contemplate, feel, remember, and innovate. In this chapter you've considered your learning style, skills and talents, personality, and life story, and even discovered at least five levels of your soul. And you've seen examples of how to greatly enhance your B-Mitzvah by connecting these aspects of yourself to your Torah portion, party, mentors, mitzvah project, and more.

The next chapter will help you plan your choices for B-Mitzvah Jewish studies from among an exciting array of options.

Chapter Four

Shaping a Meaningful Jewish Study Plan & Service

This chapter will help you to assess where you are with your Judaism and provide a basic tutorial in some of the most interesting and significant religious practices of *Bar/Bat Mitzvah* (B-Mitzvah). Your study plan will serve you best when you incorporate those aspects of Judaism that you need and want to experience and understand better. And because private instruction is customary, B-Mitzvah offers an opportunity for you to set your own learning pace and agenda.

Imagine you are invited to decide the criteria for B-Mitzvah for a colony being founded on the moon. Some good teachers have been sent along on the expedition, but now they've asked for your guidance. Their question for you is this: "Do you think someone can be ready for B-Mitzvah if she or he has never been to a Passover *seder*, sat in a *sukkah*, met the prime minister of Israel, or memorized the entire Sabbath prayer service?"

What might it take, in your opinion, for a person to qualify as a basically prepared Jew, someone you'd be ready to have come up to the Torah for B-Mitzvah and, after Shabbat, for whom you would sign on his or her certificate as a witness?

MAJOR CATEGORIES OF JUDAISM AS A SPIRITUAL PRACTICE

Add the six missing major categories of Jewish practice to this list. The answers appear on the next page.

God	
	Shabbat
Hebrew	
	Peoplehood

Not such an easy question, is it? There is no correct answer because this is both a personal and a local matter. Norms for B-Mitzvah readiness differ from community to community and have intensified quite a bit since Talmudic times. To decide what is right for you, it may help to understand how Judaism fits together as a coherent system of practices.

Complete the table on the next page to see what a rich model for living Judaism offers. Now let's consider why.

Try this: Imagine living in a world that allows no ceremonies for welcoming a new baby, making the transition from youth to adulthood, or burying a loved one. This world tolerates only one form of civilization, and this one doesn't savor or celebrate the change of seasons, is intolerant of those who take time off from work, and ignores those who cannot take care of themselves. It also forbids prayer, freedom, literature, and challenges to authority. Imagine a world with only national holidays: days off for war memorials and slain presidents or heroes. In that world neither a Passover *seder*, Hanukkah *menorah*, nor call of the shofar is allowed. Imagine a culture 100 percent determined by corporate marketing, where time is organized only for productivity.

MAJOR CATEGORIES OF JUDAISM AS A SPIRITUAL PRACTICE
(ANSWER KEY)

God	Holidays
Torah	Shabbat
Prayer	Mitzvot
Hebrew	Israel
Life-cycle events	Peoplehood

Every B-Mitzvah student is a culture holder—someone who holds the memory of an amazing way to fully celebrate life. Part of becoming an adult Jew is completing basic training for cultural leadership through knowledge of your people's history, prayers, chants, dances, stories, festivals, and other sacred practices that contribute to the art of living and caring for each other and the world.

In a page or two, we'll get specific about what you'll need to know for the B-Mitzvah ceremony itself. Before that, based on your own assessment of what is appropriate for a person to know and have experienced as a Jew in order to attain B-Mitzvah, let's take a look at where you stand.

Remember Ben and Sara from Chapter Two? Their mom and dad asked them to give thought to what they want to learn about Judaism during their B-Mitzvah preparation. They made their reflections on this a first entry in their B-Mitzvah journal with a chart for each of the categories of Judaism and an important question they each hoped to resolve during their B-Mitzvah. After reviewing Ben's chart, you can make one of your own. It is fine to have more than one question for each category.

Ben's Opening Study Questions For B-Mitzvah Preparation

God	What if someone is angry with God for bad things that happen in life? Can we talk about that?
Torah	Why are there two different Garden of Eden stories?
Prayer	Why are there so many kinds of *Kaddish* in services?
Hebrew	Where did Hebrew come from? Why do we keep it?
Life-cycle events	Why did it take so long for girls to be allowed to become *Bat Mitzvah*?
Holy Days	Do I always have to forgive? Also, I'd like to receive a shofar as a B-Mitzvah present and learn to blow it.
Shabbat	Why is Shabbat called a queen and God a king?
Mitzot	If there are 613 mitzvot, there must be a lot I've never heard of. I'd like to learn about some of those
Israel	There are many place names in my Torah portion. I'd like to see them on a map of the Middle East, learn if they still exist today, and either visit or see pictures of them.
People	Our new neighbor is a Jewish teacher from Argentina. She says our Jewish Federation has been a big help to her family. How did Jews get to South America originally? Why are they having problems, and how does the Federation know to help?

Judaism contains more of value and fascination than any one person could learn in a given lifetime. The goal at B-Mitzvah is not to try to know it all but rather to arrive at your B-Mitzvah prepared for full membership in "the tribe." On the day of your B-Mitzvah, we hope you'll feel strengthened by all you've learned and accomplished, excited about what you have developed for those who will be present on your special day; most of all, we hope you will already be imagining what you want to explore next.

Preparing For Your Ceremony

Religion is a significant part of any enduring civilization. And ceremonies such as B-Mitzvah, when conducted with meaning, spirituality, and integrity, can be hugely helpful to the human spirit. Just as Hindus, Native Americans, and others hold remarkable sacred ceremonies, we Jews do, too.

Religious ceremonies have many ritualized roles, symbols, and prayers. The service at which you will attain B-Mitzvah contains such a ceremony: the Torah service. If you are to experience the most powerful effects of this ceremony, you first need to be able to recognize the drama that is unfolding and the meaning behind each symbol.

Note: from here on in this chapter, you may find material both new and familiar. Start your study process out now by highlighting new material so that you can easily return to it for deeper study.

Take a look at the table below. Do you know the origin or meaning of any of the symbols that are listed? Read on to learn the answers; they may prove to be rather interesting and surprising. Then return to complete the table with your new knowledge.

SACRED SYMBOLISM IN SERVICES	
Fill in the right-hand column with what you think the symbol in the left-hand column means or represents	
Symbol	**What This Means or Represents**
Crown on the Torah	
Bells on the crown	
Embroidered Torah cover	
Wooden staves that hold and roll the Torah scroll	
Breastplate that hangs over the Torah	
Bimah, raised platform for the Torah table and leader's stand	
Ark, cabinet for the Torah, the *aron kodesh*	
Yad, hand-shaped pointer for reading Torah (so the ink won't wear off)	

What Is The Meaning Of Shabbat Symbols And Practices?

Imagine it is your B-Mitzvah day and time for you to go up to the Torah. You are about to become an adult witness and participant in the reading and interpretation of Torah. Go ahead, approach the ark; it represents the ark of the covenant, in which the Israelites carried the carved tablets with the Ten Commandments in the wilderness. The doors of the ark are opened. You will cross a threshold in your life as an elder or leader of the community places the Torah in your arms. The sacred mantle of leadership is upon you.

Experience the weight, feel, and appearance of the Torah. Most likely it will be dressed in an embroidered cover. (Sephardic communities encase their Torahs in beautifully painted cases.) The Torah is dressed according to the garments of Aaron, the high priest, who wore a blue robe embroidered with pomegranates alternating with real golden bells along the bottom (Exodus 28:34). Folklore says this fruit has 613 seeds, which is the total number of mitzvot according to Maimonides.

The forehead of the high priest was crowned by a piece of hammered gold with the words *kodesh l'Adonai*, "holy to God," engraved upon it. When they can afford to do so, communities commission crowns of precious metal to place atop the Torah scroll. The crown is also said to symbolize the metaphor for God as *melech*, "king," which can be understood as a metaphor for the governing principles of creation.

Gold bells dangled from the hem of the high priest's robe. The crown of your Torah likely has tiny bells that tinkle when it is lifted. The community would be alerted by the bells to the presence of the high priest in their midst. Commentators also imagined the high priest's experience in the section of the temple known as the holy of holies as so wonderfully intense that his soul might leave his body in order to cling to this experience of God. So they wondered if the bells might be a signal system, alerting temple workers to run into the holy of holies to save the high priest's life if the bells ceased ringing.

The Torah in your arms may be wearing a silver breastplate. The high priest wore one for ritual occasions. It was embedded with twelve stones, representing each of the tribes, and it had a secret compartment used as a tool for decision making.

The Torah scroll is mounted on two wooden rollers that are its handles. These are called the *eitz chayyim*, the Tree of Life. You may remember the trees that stood in the Garden of Eden: the Tree of Knowledge and the Tree of Life. That Tree of Life has traveled through time and become the words of Torah. You are holding the Tree of Life in your arms.

The *yad*, a pointer, often made of precious metal and shaped like a hand with one finger pointing, will likely be hanging over one of the *eitz chayyim* poles. The pointer's shape recalls what the Torah says (Exodus 32:18), that the Ten Commandments were written in stone with the "finger of God."

You see, all of your life you have been traveling toward Mount Sinai, which is symbolized by the *bimah*, the stage or reader's platform. At your B-Mitzvah, you will make *aliyah*, ascend, as Moses did, in order to bring down Torah for your people.

Receiving Torah can change your life; it has for our people. What a wonder that the Israelites did not replicate the system of pharaoh, taskmasters, and slaves out there in the wilderness! Instead, they entered the promised land after a journey from slavery to freedom based on what was then a radical new system for living that today we know as Torah.

Tip

Jewish Vision Quest
To step away from the crowd, pour your heart out to God, and listen for guidance is a basic right and essential practice with which to become comfortable. It doesn't even matter if you believe there is a God listening to you for this to be a valuable experience.

Take a trip into nature for a Jewish Vision Quest, whatever your age. Here's how it works:

1. Find a safe place in nature where no one can hear you and you cannot get lost. Bring water and tissues.
2. Begin to talk out loud to God. Share whatever you are feeling, longing for, wondering about, frustrated with, working through, astonished by, delighted and grateful for. Keep speaking; don't stop.
3. If you run out of words, say "lah-lah-lah," "oi, yoi, yoi," or various syllables until another round of material comes up for expression.
4. Keep doing this until you are truly empty. For some people a physical act such as breaking sticks helps, too.
5. When you are empty of material, sit or wander a short distance and experience a warm silence. An answer will come to you in some way, either now or over the next days. It may come in the form of a symbol—an animal, plant, or a soft voice inside of you—or it may be carried on the wind or in many other ways.

Depending on your issue, you might want to have a mentor help you make sense of your experience afterward. If you do this as a group or class experience, create a debriefing time for those who wish to share.

This practice is called *hitbodedut*, "making yourself alone" with God. Hannah goes into the sanctuary to do this when she is sad over being childless (I Samuel 1:10–20). Moses is always heading up a mountain filled with the stresses of his duties and finding renewed vision at the top.

Rabbi Nachman of Breslov taught this form of personal prayer over two hundred years ago. With practice you can do this silently inside of yourself, anywhere, to receive relief, comfort, and insight.

You will carry that radical document, Torah, the record of our people's journey from slavery to freedom, through the community on your B-Mitzvah. It contains the first known guidelines for how to create a society based on respect, freedom, and love within healthy social structures and guidelines.

Faces from the story of your life—family, community, teachers, and friends—will be looking at you as you turn to face them with the sacred scroll in your arms. They will see and hear you in a new light on your B-Mitzvah day, the light of Torah.

Receiving The Light

Most of the good things in life involve a process of preparation. For example, a tennis player doesn't leap up from bed to take the first stroke of a game; she begins with a series of warm-up exercises that stretch each muscle group. Each stage of a service is designed to warm you up for prayer within yourself and on behalf of others. Following is a map of the intent of the stages of the Shabbat morning service, the time when most B-Mitzvah ceremonies take place. In addition to needing at least one edition of the full Jewish scriptures for your studies, you will also need a well-designed siddur, prayer book; every denomination publishes at least one; their websites can be found in the Resources section at the end of this book.

Preparing Your Service Booklet
B-Mitzvah families often prepare a booklet of creative readings and explanations of the service and Torah reading. Those designing a B-Mitzvah that will be held independently of a congregation generally include all the major prayers, along with their translations and transliterations in this booklet, so that it can serve as the prayer book. These also serve as a gift for those who attend to take home for further contemplation.

1. Begin by creating a computer file or shirt box labeled for each major part of the service. As you come across possible

interpretive readings and graphics, save them in the appropriate file.

2. Seek out a Hebrew-English word-processing program. Often such programs have a traditional Hebrew siddur and Torah already in their databases; you can easily format a booklet using them, as well as insert color graphics and photos.

3. Customize your effort as much as possible. Are you a doodler? Create borders. A cartoonist? Reveal something about the prayers or the story in your Torah portion. Do you have friends who are poets? Ask them to address a theme or prayer as their gift to you, and include their work in the booklet.

4. Many who attend will be in the dark about Jewish practices. To prevent awkward moments, include in your booklet explanations and guides to practice.

5. Create a yizkor or memorial page dedicated to those who have died before your special day.

6. Create an appreciation page for your B-Mitzvah planning and preparation team. Remember family, friends, tutors, clergy, artists—everyone who helped you reach your goals.

7. Remember that Hebrew reads from right to left, so booklets for Jewish prayer, even when there are transliterations and translations, are meant to be printed and read from back to front. To bind your booklet you'll need extra margin off-set space; create that with your formatting, and remember about the back-to-front when setting up page number locations. That's important to tell your printer as well.

Consider involving a few capable guests in taking roles or parts in the service. Some communities welcome this approach. Because not all guests will be Jewish, learn which parts of a service are covenantal and only appropriately led by a Jew and which parts are universal or lend themselves to supplementary material such as poems, singing, or dance. Norms for this vary widely among communities; Be sure those with parts sit in the front row to save "travel" time.

Once you have the printed service booklets, be sure to create annotated copies with highlighted sections that bear each reader's name. Add colored notes that stick out from the pages that each reader needs to know about. Note any stage directions that are important, such as, "rise from your seat and read," or "come up to the front with the three readers prior to you; you each have a paragraph to read; yours is first."

Write participants' names clearly on the cover, and have their booklets on a special reception table outside the room where your service will take place. Have someone at that table note who has arrived, and make sure the participant receives his or her booklet.

Prepare several copies of a comprehensively annotated service booklet, with the full names of readers. So that you can honor them, add pronunciation guides if you need them; mark who is saying and doing what very clearly. Have a comprehensive copy ready for the B-Mitzvah student, any clergy who will be on the *bimah*, tutors, mentors, and other key players.

Plan ushers who will ask arriving guests if they are familiar with a Jewish service and who will offer to seat them with someone who can help softly interpret the goings on.

Finding Personal Meaning in the Prayer Service

To transform services from lots of words into personal meaning, go over the map of the Shabbat morning prayer service, which will be helpful as you page through your siddur. Note on the following "map" how the early service integrates body, mind, and spirit as the first phase of prayer. Only after warming up with the energy of the psalms is there a collective experience of prayer in which the community responds together in the Borchu. Review each important stage.

Because Hebrew is a highly poetic, nuanced language, many shades of interpretation are possible for any verse. That is one reason the prayers never get old for those who understand them. You might take on learning a few more prayers in depth as part of your preparation plan; ask your teacher(s) to work with you, to show you how to find the many shades of meaning.

Beyond the individual prayers is your innermost personal prayer. Notice how on the map, at the apex of the service, is the *amidah*, a time of rising in silent contemplation of your life in order to find and express the prayer of your heart. This means listening within yourself for what you feel, notice, hope, and need. The prophet Elijah taught the importance of not assuming that the loudest voice you hear is the most important.

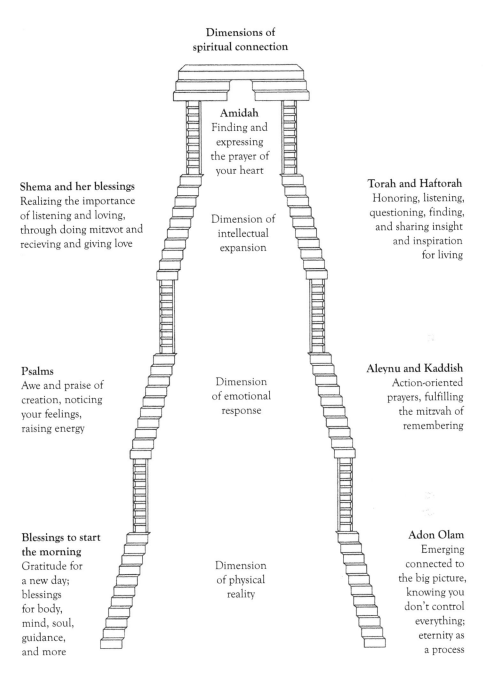

Dimensions of
spiritual connection

Amidah
Finding and
expressing
the prayer of
your heart

Shema and her blessings
Realizing the importance
of listening and loving,
through doing mitzvot and
recieving and giving love

Dimension of
intellectual
expansion

Torah and Haftorah
Honoring, listening,
questioning, finding,
and sharing insight
and inspiration
for living

Psalms
Awe and praise of
creation, noticing
your feelings,
raising energy

Dimension
of emotional
response

Aleynu and Kaddish
Action-oriented
prayers, fulfilling
the mitzvah of
remembering

**Blessings to start
the morning**
Gratitude for
a new day;
blessings
for body,
mind, soul,
guidance,
and more

Dimension
of physical
reality

Adon Olam
Emerging
connected to
the big picture,
knowing you
don't control
everything;
eternity as
a process

**Map of the Shabbat Morning Prayer Service. Inspired by the Meta-Siddur
teachings of Rabbi David Wolfe-Blank z"1.**

Tip

Finding the Prayer of Your Heart

When seeking the prayer of your heart, it can help to first clear a space by noticing your breath and following it. Sit comfortably with eyes softly focused, asking, "How am I?" Anything that comes up, honor it by gently imagining putting it out on a table, and then see if there's more that wants to come. Don't investigate each thing; just let a full inner inventory happen.

Happy or challenging items may come up. If the feeling is about something difficult, beware of senses or voices within that carry guilt, shame, or say "should" and "if only." Without giving these voices extra weight, let them take their place on the shelf along with the stiller, softer voices. Elijah (1 Kings 19:11-12) discovers God is not in the whirlwind, the earthquake, or the fire, but in the stillness where you can hear a small soft voice.

When you feel empty of life matters to be placed on the counter of your life during this exercise, sit quietly; be with yourself. Your body will speak to you, perhaps via a glow of happiness. Or you could feel like dancing or purring, or sense a tugging, hurt, or turmoil somewhere inside. Pick one sense; it might be murky, unclear right now, and rather than thinking about it, feel its effect on your body and spirit. Gently sit with the sensation and where it is within you. Now gradually become curious about it.

Is there one word, sense, or image that comes up about this matter? What quality helps this place to be better described? Go back and forth between it and the word or sense you have about it until you have a way to describe it.

Now ask this "sense" what it needs. Perhaps it's a sense that wants to be expressed as a prayer of gratitude for life. Or perhaps the sense wants a change from you; listen for what is needed. Ask it what it wants from you. Ask what if it became OK and what's in the way of that happening. Welcome with patience this prayer your body is helping you formulate.

Now you might imagine whispering your prayer of what is needed and wanted to happen into the ear of the Cosmos, or you might take out your B-Mitzvah journal and write a memo to God explaining what you've noticed and what you hope will happen. For example, Sara, from Chapter One, shared with us a piece that she wrote at summer camp: "Dear God, I wish I could go home today." "Dear God, please help the other kids to like me." "Dear God, please give me the courage to sit next to Karen. I think she'd be a cool friend." And Ben, at the same camp, wrote, "Thank you God for the fun I had today. I feel so happy and full of life!"

When doing this at home or synagogue, you might want to put on a *tallit*, a prayer shawl. Sometimes you'll see a person place her *tallit* over her head at services or when praying at home; this is to create private, sacred space. (We will discuss the *tallit* at more length later in this chapter.)

This guide is based on a method the author was privileged to learn from Kye Nelson and from Dr. Gene Gendlin, author of Focusing and founder of Focusing.org, where you can receive guidance in deepening the applications of this method to living.

A service leader needs internal preparation in order to be most effective at receiving Torah and offering it in a meaningful way to the community. Each prayer in the traditional *amidah* is a springboard to helping you focus your personal prayers. (Rabbi Marcia Prager has a beautiful set of *amidah* cards that reveal this process; there's a link to her work and other spiritually innovative rabbis and cantors at Ohalah.org and ALEPH.org.) Even before finding meaning in each part of the *amidah* comes the prayer skill of how to use the silence of the *amidah*.

Sharing The Light

Becoming B-Mitzvah means listening beyond what you want for yourself. It is a time to remember what is on the plate of the lives of those

WHO IS IN THE MINYAN (INNER CIRCLE) OF YOUR LIFE?	
Who is in the *minyan* of your life? And what is going on in their lives that you might pray for on their behalf during your *amidah* prayer on your B-Mitzvah day? Look at the two examples and in your journal add your *minyan* and your own potential prayers for them.	
Name	**Your Prayer for This Person**
Aunt Annie	She's been so sad since Uncle Jack died three years ago. Please help her see how much I and the other cousins love her and miss going out on the town with her. Help her heart heal; give her the strength to come to my B-Mitzvah and see the whole family. Please!
Dan, my brother	Dan is so excited about his new job. What a great gift to find a job that uses so many of his talents. May he get along great with everyone there, and may it turn out to be just right for him!

immediately around you and those in the world as a whole. Then you can fully pray for what is needed, hoped for, and appreciated.

What prayers do you have for those in your life, in this world? How do you go about forming such prayers? This starts with recognizing who really is important to you in the *minyan* of your life. To help you decide, please complete Who Is in the *Minyan* of Your Life.

Who do you show up for in life, and who shows up for you? The spiritual meaning of a *minyan* is more than the traditional ten people needed as a quorum to hold a service. Your *minyan* is also the inner circle of your life, those who not only care about you but who also help when needed and those for whom you care. These are the first members of your guest list and the faces you will most eagerly seek on the day of your B-Mitzvah.

Now you, like the high priest of old and the rabbi and cantor of today, can face your community as one who is *kodesh l'Adonai*, filled with the holiness of Becoming. A person's mind clears and heart opens after such a prayer sequence. When you step up to the ark to take on the mantle of leadership, even your voice will sound different because of all the feelings about family and friends that will enrich the sound of who you are. You are going to give them a present, your self, your participation in the "tribe," your reading of the sacred text with care after great preparation, and your vision of what they need to hear to help them connect to meaning for living through the text.

The Importance Of Your Name

You will be called to the Torah by your sacred name. Having a Jewish name that rings true for you is very important whether you are the B-Mitzvah student, parent of the student, or a guest being given the honor of an *aliyah*. Names hold power and meaning. If you have a Hebrew name, now is the time to connect deeply with its meaning. If you don't, we'll show how you can get one.

Names can add energy to your sense of self, fall flat, or be draining. If you have a Jewish name that you don't appreciate, you can change it easily by being called to the Torah with your new name and having your final blessing including mention of the taking of this name. Or if there's a family story behind that name and changing it would be super "sensitive," you might decide to make it a middle Hebrew name and put your preferred one in front of it. And if you don't have a Jewish name yet, you need to find one now.

For a while rabbis and cantors were stopping people from using Yiddish names up at the Torah, even though in Europe before the war this was common. Although Hebrew became extremely important with the rebirth of Israel as a sovereign state with its own language, as the Yiddish-speaking generations are passing away, many realize that Yiddish names are also holy and need to be preserved. Today most communities accept that you can be called to Torah with a Hebrew or Yiddish name.

A person is called up to the Torah with a personal Jewish name as well as the Jewish names of his or her parents, or in the case of converts, in the name of Sarah and Abraham, the first Jewish family. For example:

Sara's name is already a Hebrew name, so she will be called to the Torah as Sara *bat* (daughter of) Ari (her dad's Hebrew name) *v'* (and) Malka (her mom's Hebrew name). She will hear herself called by the command: "*Ta'amode* [arise] *Sara bat Ari v'Malka!*"

Ben is short for Benjamin, which in Hebrew is Benyamin (Hebrew has no J sound), so he will be called to the Torah as Benyamin *ben* (son of) Ari (his dad's Hebrew name) *v'* (and) Malka (his mom's Hebrew name). He will hear himself called up by the command: "*Ya'amode* [arise] *Benyamin ben Ari v'Malka!*"

In intermarried families the Jewish parent's name will usually be used after the student's, although sometimes both parents' names are used because, in fairness, they are the parents! In the latter case, one parent won't have a Jewish name, so his or her English first name can be used. What about a Jewish parent who hasn't had a B-Mitzvah and doesn't have a Jewish name? What a great project it will be to select one and adopt it in preparation for this special day. A forgotten or lost Jewish name can sometimes be found by interviewing family, looking at grave stones, or checking stored religious documents or inside the cover of your old Hebrew school books.

Most important, once you have a Jewish name, B-Mitzvah is an important time to get close to its meaning, so that when you are called to Torah, everything about your self comes up with you.

If you are contemplating a new Hebrew name, try it on!

- Write yourself a letter addressed to the possible name.
- Imagine your friends calling you by this name.
- Ask a few people in your life to call you by the name for a few hours so that you can see how it feels.

When the name is right, your whole body will resonate "Yes, that's me!"

Find out in what verses of Torah and prayer the name you are drawn to appears. A keyword search on-line can prove fascinating and

Tip

Choosing Your Jewish Sacred Name
Jewish name choices are most often of these types:

- Characters from the Bible and Jewish history
  Moshe = Moses; Rivka = Rebecca; Shimon = Simon
- Names from nature
  Ari = lion; Hadassah = myrtle; Shoshana = lily
- Desired qualities of character or feeling
  Bahira = clarity; Tikva = hope; *Simcha* = happiness

It's also helpful to know that although Sephardic Jews have the tradition of honoring a living member of the family by taking on that person's name, Ashkenazi Jews carefully reserve this as an act of memorial.

sometimes sobering. There may be an important message embedded in that verse for you, the name might prove to have connections you do not want.

In the back of *The Complete Art Scroll Siddur* (Artscroll.com), you will find an alphabetical listing of selected verses from the Torah. One custom is to look up a verse that begins with the first and ends with the last letter of your Hebrew name and see if there is a message in it for you. It is particularly traditional to do this at the end of the *amidah* during services.

Drop by a synagogue library, or resource room at a Jewish community center or Board or Bureau of Jewish Education. The staff can offer dictionaries and resources that explain the meaning of many Jewish names. (Some websites give inaccurate name translations, be sure to check with a rabbi.)

When you find the right name, wear it! Think how happy it will make someone for you to suggest their B-Mitzvah gift to you might be your Jewish name on a necklace or ring, or a donation to a good cause in your honor and in your Hebrew name.

The Cosmic Drama

An important part of B-Mitzvah readiness is learning that on Shabbat an even bigger drama is going on than your B-Mitzvah and the Torah reading. Did you know that giving a *d'var Torah* on Shabbat is considered to be a wedding present for God? Go take the quick test on the next page for the fun of it.

Now let's take one more giant step back into the sacred drama of Judaism. Shabbat has the model and meaning of a wedding. So who's getting married? In a way, you are. To our ancestors the idea of "bride" meant awaiting a very special change in your life, feeling fully alive, excited, fresh, clear, pure, and receptive. Renewing this kind of feeling, bringing the "bride" inside was their favorite metaphor for Shabbat. The Jewish idea is that as the week wears on, a person gets tired from ceaseless activities; mistakes start to happen more often, relationships can get strained. We may start cutting corners in order to get things done. The glow of your best self can become dim when you need rest and reenergizing.

So the Friday night service begins with six psalms, one to help remove the "veil" of stress from each of the six days of the week before Shabbat. Then comes the seventh psalm, *L'cha Dodi*, which welcomes the feeling of Shabbat coming toward you using the metaphor of the bride: *boe-ee kallah, boe-ee kallah,* "Welcome, bride!" we sing as we turn to invite the glow of Shabbat inside the community, the synagogue, inside ourselves.

So if the reenergizing, intimate feeling of Shabbat happening is the bride, then what is the groom? The groom happens when we remember there is structure to the universe that we can trust, an amazing unity of design that our ancestors intuited and that scientists are uncovering every day. In Judaism the governing principles, *melech*, the king-like

FINDING MEANING IN SHABBAT PRACTICES	
Symbol	Meaning or Origin in Torah
Shabbat as a bride	
Two candles	
White candles and tablecloths	
Dressing up for Shabbat	
Six psalms before L'cha Dodi at Friday night services	
Blessing wine, saying *Kiddush*	
Giving a *d'var Torah*	
Having an *oneg* after services	
A braided *Havdalah* candle	

aspects of creation are one face of God; they are in part revealed in the structure we turn to for inspiration, the Torah, which is symbolically wearing a crown.

And so another face of God is the flow and energy of creation called *Malkah*, "queen," which when united with *Melech*, "king," brings the structure of creation fully alive. This allows for intimacy and a sense of God as presence, a quality of God experience our people also know by the name *Shechinah* and Shabbat. Shabbat is a cosmic wedding, a weekly recommitment ceremony to re-soul a person with practices that dissolve the illusion a hard week can give of the world being fragmented. On Shabbat we reclaim the core meaning of the *Shema*, *Adonai Echad*, all is One.

Now that you know that Shabbat is modeled on a wedding, can you guess why Shabbat candles, tablecloths, and even clothes are, by tradition, white? Indeed, because white is the color of the eggshell, of a new fresh sheet in the Torah of your life; this is a white wedding. To give visual pleasure to the bride and groom, people dress up at a wedding. On Shabbat one tries to feel comfortable and look one's best.

So who are the wedding guests? That's a paradox: each person is both the bride and a guest. In synagogue the guests are the congregation, and the reception afterward of usually cakes and drinks is called an *oneg*, meaning pleasure, and represents the royal wedding reception. The ritual is repeated at home, too; Shabbat dinner is the wedding reception, and it's a mitzvah to have guests. Many expand this mitzvah with the pleasure of fresh flowers for their Shabbat table decorations.

When are the wedding vows? The potential to bring new life into the world is a core mitzvah of both Shabbat and a Jewish wedding. Wine symbolizes the life-force in Judaism. Just as at every Jewish wedding there is a blessing over the wine, which symbolizes the life-force, every Shabbat we say a prayer called *Kiddush*, which blesses the holiness of life, the love and desire we have for it, and the life-giving power of new beginnings. A Jewish wedding finishes with seven blessings, and in the Talmud the *Kiddush* originally had seventy words, so *Kiddush* symbolizes seven to the power of ten blessings for this reconnection of your soul with the meaning and experience of being fully alive.

Lighting Shabbat candles, leading *Kiddush*, and the blessing over the gift of the rather amazing transformation of what was once star dust into bread, called *Hamotzi*, are practices that the B-Mitzvah student often undertakes; you will find them in most every prayer book. And remember, no weekday bread will do; Shabbat is a *challah*-day!

A slave would have to work every day, but Judaism is designed as an antidote to slavery. Shabbat is a celebration of life, a cosmic wedding— and on this occasion, also of your B-Mitzvah. It is also a honeymoon from homework and other weekly efforts. So, of course, your B-Mitzvah and Shabbat offer lots of time for partying, getting filled with great food, socializing, and dancing joyfully.

Tradition

And God told Moses, "Speak to the children of Israel, and guide them throughout their generations to make fringes on the corners of their garments."

—Numbers 15:37–40

You will see them [the fringes] and remember all God's mitzvot and do them.

—Numbers 15:39

You've likely heard of chaos theory, where a butterfly that flutters its wings in China sets in motion a chain of changes that one day affect something in your part of the world. Our ancestors have always believed that about the practice of Shabbat—that Shabbat is a cosmic wedding, with benefits inside of you and far beyond you. Just think of many things that might have been that may possibly change because your family comes to share the special Shabbat of your B-Mitzvah with you.

Something is missing from this wedding. What about presents? Are there wedding presents for the king, and Shabbat, the queen? Your *d'var Torah* is the wedding present. Tradition holds that whenever a new interpretation of Torah is given, inside the scroll the crowns on the letters that are shaped like flames begin to twinkle in appreciation.

Learning to use, care for, and benefit from the major personal Jewish ritual objects is an important part of B-Mitzvah preparation. The major items involved are *tallitot*, *kippot*, and *tefillin*.

Tallit

The *tallit* is a four-cornered prayer shawl with specially knotted fringes, called *tzitzit*, worn as a reminder to live a mitzvah-centered life. A *tallit* is a portable spiritual home in which you can wrap yourself at home, in synagogue, or when you are away on adventures and desire time for prayer, reflection, or healing from a sore spot in your life.

A person generally selects or receives his or her first full *tallit* during the process of preparation for B-Mitzvah. Some Jews, from early childhood on, wear a lightweight *tallit* called a *tallit kattan*, "little *tallit*," under their clothes; and others prefer the full shawl-style *tallit* for prayer and special occasions in life.

• A Jewish wedding canopy is often a large *tallit*, a canopy of spirit, held over the couple on four poles.
• A Jewish person is buried wearing a *tallit*. One corner is symbolically cut off; in some communities only males are buried this way
• An old *tallit* that is unsightly, torn, or unusable gets donated to the synagogue or a Judaic library and will be used to wrap worn-out or superfluous documents like photocopies with the sacred YHVH name of God, pronounced *Adonai*, on them in Hebrew script so that they can be buried with dignity in a *geniza*, a Jewish cemetery section set aside for this purpose.
• Sometimes when a child becomes sick, the parents wrap her or him in a *tallit* and pace the floors as they pray for healing.
• The Yemenite Jews have a practice of wearing an all-black *tallit* at prayer during a period of mourning. Some Jews have an all-white *tallit* to wear on Yom Kippur, symbolizing rebirth. Recently, *tallitot* (plural) have appeared in many-colored varieties throughout the world.
• A full *tallit* is never worn in a bathroom; it is a sacred item. (Nor are *tefillin*; a *kippah* can be worn everywhere.)

- People who are leading services often wear a full *tallit*; all others wear a full *tallit* only at morning services, and some orthodox Jewish men wear only a *tallit kattan* until they are married and then receive a full *tallit*, often as a wedding present. (See Bmitzvah.org for a guide to traditions about the meaning of the knots and windings and rare exceptions to the above.)

Finding a Tallit Just Right for You
Local Judaica stores, many websites, synagogue gift shops, and custom-*tallit* makers await your visit. You can buy a *tallit* ready-made, or order one, or make one yourself by choosing a favorite color, fabric, style, decoration, and texture. Some *tallit* makers will offer the option of shipping yours with the fringes not yet attached so that you can do the knotting as a family or personal ritual.

Tradition

Women wearing *tzitzit* is a revival of the Torah's guidance for all to put fringes on their garments. This practice had lapsed by the time of the Maimonides' twelfth-century compilation of Jewish practice known as the *Mishneh Torah*. The *Talmud*, the authoritative, fourth-century compilation of rabbinic discussions on Jewish laws, ethics, customs, legends, and stories in *Tractate Menahot* 43a, reports that Reb Yehudah attached fringes to the aprons of women in his household: "All must observe the law of *tzitzit*, Cohanim, Levites and Israelites, converts, women and slaves." This section also records one scholar, Reb Simeon, as declaring women not to be obligated to wear *tzitzit*.

Putting Your Tallit On and Away

Hold the *tallit* so that the decorative collar, called the *atarah*, is facing you. Often these have the blessing for wearing a *tallit* on them, a verse from Torah, a prayer of deep meaning, or a decoration. Let yourself feel what it means to enter this fabric sukkah, a shelter of peace.

Some people kiss the *tallit* at this point, the way you might put a kiss on a mezuzah, realizing you are crossing a threshold (the root word of *Adonai*— "Lord," *ehden*, means windowsill or threshold) with the intention of creating sacred space.

Recite the blessing: *Baruch ata adonai eloheynu melech ha-olam asher kidshanu b'mitzvotav v'tzivanu l'hitateyf ba-tzitzit.*—Blessed is our God, Governing Principle of the universe that makes us holy through guiding us to do the mitzvah of wrapping in fringes, the symbol of the mitzvot.

Holding your *tallit* like a cape by the *atarah*, fling it up and around and over your shoulders. Some wear it like a cape; others fold it into a neat column of fabric; some wear it like a shawl. If a *tallit* is very large, it is customary to flip the corners up onto your shoulders. It is very helpful to have a *tallit* clip, which is two alligator clips and a tiny chain or ribbon that will keep your *tallit* from slipping all the way off during the movements of prayer and Torah reading.

When it is time to take your *tallit* off, fold it gently and return it to a protective pouch. Caution: *Tzitzit* don't wash well, so dry cleaning is a must. The fringes need to be covered with foil when going through the process, or they will fray. Should you have a *tallit* with worn fringes, just clip them off and tie new ones on. They can be purchased at most Judaica shops.

What Color Is Your Kippah?

The little round beanie Jews often wear to pray is called a *kippah* in Hebrew, *yarmulke* in Yiddish, and skullcap in English. For most contemporary Jews, the decision to wear a *kippah* all day is a religious choice. So if you are wearing a *kippah* and get attracted to doing something that would not be good for you or others, you might remember you have a *kippah* on; just that Godly "tug" of what you really

Tip

Creating a Tzitzit-Tying Ritual

Sara Harwin, a Judaica fabric artist (Harwinstudios.com), introduced the author to the idea of a blessing ritual for the tying of the fringes onto your *tallit*.

1. Take the *tallit*, either a new one without fringes yet applied or an older one onto which you want to put new fringes, and drape it over the B-Mitzvah student.
2. Have someone or several special persons in your life on hand to help tie the knots. (Although not difficult, this is detail-intensive. You can find a full guide to tying *tzitzit* and the meaning of the number of knots at Bmitzvah.org.)
3. Ask those coming to bring a blessing they wish to give the B-Mitzvah student; this will become part of your memory of preparing this *tallit*. These blessings can be prepared in advance and also provided on paper to the student for inclusion in a B-Mitzvah memory book. A blessing might sound like this: "May you be blessed to find wonderful Jewish communities that you enjoy greatly throughout your lifetime!"
4. For each of the four corners of the *tallit*, assign the blessing individual or blessing team. Decide which is preferable, to receive the blessings before the winding and knotting for that corner or after, and begin. As an option you might reserve one corner for the student to ask for his or her own most desired blessings. Take turns reflecting the student's desired blessing back to her. Leader, inquire if each blessing feels right. Adjust if needed. Now all present can respond: Amen!

believe in may stop you from getting into trouble. Others prefer to wear a *kippah* only for ritual situations, such as mealtime blessings, during private prayer, while at services, or during a religious ritual.

The Israelites of biblical times and Jews even as recently as medieval times did not wear a *kippah*. This practice has evolved relatively recently. Covering the head is first spoken about in connection with the official garments of the high priest in Exodus 28:4, 37, 40. He wore a type of head ornament called a *mitznefet*; the ordinary priests had a kind of hat, *migba'at*. In the books of Samuel, Jeremiah, and Esther, we learn that people in mourning would cover their heads and veil their faces, a custom that continued into Greek and Roman times. The Talmud reports that some who felt great awe for the experience of a Divine Presence in the world would also veil their faces and cover their heads, especially while praying or studying.

It gradually became an optional custom for Torah scholars to cover their heads. For those who would lead services and give the priestly blessing, a head covering became normal among the Jews in Babylonia. The great medieval commentator known as the Maharsha ruled that wearing a head covering during prayer was optional, although Maimonides equated an uncovered head with a person who does not take living seriously enough. Not until the seventeenth century did writers describe a difference between Christians and Jews as that of Jewish men covering their heads during prayer.

Kippot are available in endless shapes, sizes, designs, and colors. A person's choice of *kippah* communicates something: a big plain black one usually means the person lives a very observant, traditional life; a tiny colorful handmade one often signifies an active, spiritual, liberal Jew. Or maybe someone was just attracted to a particular *kippah* and chose it or made it by hand. Some people have bowls of kippot at home for guests to borrow and to match with outfits. What color would you like your B-Mitzvah *kippah* to be?

There are many ways to express being Jewish. If it's not your family's usual practice, wearing a *kippah* for a while—in public, during study, prayer, or meals—is a nice religious experiment to try during your B-Mitzvah preparation year(s). You might write in your journal about

Tradition

Rabbi Honah ben Joshua never walked four cubits [about six feet] with an uncovered head, for he used to say, "The *Shechinah*, [God's] presence, resides above my head."

—Talmud *Kiddushin* 31a

how wearing a *kippah* changes how you experience the world and how the world reacts to you.

It takes courage to wear a *kippah* in some parts of the world; in a few neighborhoods in Israel, some Jews will become angry and aggressive at seeing a woman wearing one. Remember, Judaism does not want you to follow a practice that could put your life at risk. Putting your *kippah* in your pocket if it could result in any danger to you, or wearing a hat instead, is fine. The Torah says we are to live by our traditions, not die by them.

Must Everyone Wear A Kippah And Tallit At Services?

There are many regional and denominational variations about the wearing of a *tallit* and *kippah*. You'll see non-Jews being asked to wear kippot in certain synagogues, and in others someone will try to prevent them from doing so. Politicians of all stripes usually pop a *kippah* on when they come through the door of a synagogue. For a non-Jew it is neither necessary to wear one, nor some kind of offense or sin to do so. Customarily, a married Orthodox Jewish woman will cover her hair with a scarf, hat, or a wig and wear clothing that covers as much of her body as possible, because she saves viewing of her physical beauty for her husband, a mitzvah called *tzinius*, "modesty."

On occasion well-intentioned congregants will try to enforce local customs about *tallit* and *kippah* because they mistakenly think such local practices are part of Jewish law. Most communities no longer create barriers to women participating in the mitzvah of *tallit* or wearing a *kippah* if they so choose. Well-instructed ushers at your service can softly tell arriving guests whatever custom your community prefers. Where local custom allows for the mitzvah of hospitality to prevail, it's most welcoming to guests to allow them to choose for themselves.

A nice B-Mitzvah memory and gift for your guests is created by ordering or crocheting custom kippot so that everyone who desires to will have one to wear and take home. Be sure to put a bowl of hairpins out to help hold the *kippah* on; contrary to what some people think, Jews don't have Velcro on the tops of our heads! Larger crocheted kippot work better for bald folks. Taking on the mitzvah of wearing a *tallit* for morning prayer is also a very personal decision. Again, it's a gesture of hospitality to have some extra *tallitot* for those who forgot theirs or who feel inspired to try.

Exploring Mezuzah And Tefillin

The prayers inside of a mezuzah are about the importance of listening, loving, and doing so by following the mitzvot. Traditionally, Jews place a mezuzah on every doorway in a home except for the bathroom. Transitioning from one space to another means noticing your mood, thinking about how you will affect others, and making a choice about how you will act in the next space you enter. Keep in mind that a doorway is a threshold—*ehden*, an *Adonai* space. Crossing a threshold that has a mezuzah is a reminder to bring holiness into the room.

B-Mitzvah is an important time to engage in the mitzvah of mezuzah, particularly on the one space you control the most, your own room. If a mezuzah has already been hung on the doorway to your bedroom and the casing now seems too immature for you, you can save the scroll inside, pick out or make a new cover, and create a mezuzah-hanging ritual for your personal sacred space. (Visit ReclaimingJudaism. org; under Life-Cycle Rituals, you will find a full guide to holding a mezuzah-hanging ritual and party.)

Meditation is an important part of Judaism, the wearing of *tefillin* is a morning meditation practice for every day except Shabbat. This practice is usually first introduced into a person's life during B-Mitzvah studies. Although to those unfamiliar with them *tefillin* can look pretty strange, the practice is actually quite wonderful.

The boxes on the *tefillin* are each called a *bayit*, a house, which, like the mezuzah, contain tiny handwritten scrolls with verses of the *Shema* and other blessings from the Torah. The boxes are then attached to leather straps, each knotted differently so that you can encircle the crown of your head and wind the other around your weaker or non-dominant arm.

The same verses are in each box, but the ones on the arm *tefillin*, known as the *shel yad*, are on one parchment, and those for the head, the *shel rosh*, are written by a scribe on four individual parchments, each of which gets its own room in the *bayit*, the houselike box.

Tradition

In the paragraph after the *Shema* comes the section that most clearly describes the basis for *tefillin*: "you shall bind them for a sign upon your arm and they will be for frontlets between your eyes" (Deuteronomy 6:8). *Tefillin* also contain the verses Deuteronomy 6:4–9, 11:13–21; Exodus 13:1–10 and 13:11–16.

Finding Buried Treasure

A little child of maybe seven, while exploring the basement of her suburban home, found a curious item, a velvet bag containing little boxes with long black leather straps attached to them. Hauling them upstairs, she asked her father if she could use the straps for a craft project.

Her father took the package from her hands and drew the objects out tenderly. "I have not used these since the beginning of World War II! These are called *tefillin*," he explained. "They contain handwritten scrolls with verses from the Torah about love and the importance of keeping the mitzvot as a way of showing love.

"During my term of service in World War II, the horrors I saw and experienced left me angry with God, people, and myself. Because of my army experiences, I stopped using these." He took them from her hands, saying, "These need to be put away in a more appropriate place."

When the young girl began to prepare for *Bat Mitzvah*, she saw *tefillin* on the list of items to bring to class. Showing the list to her father, she wondered how he would react.

"Just a minute, I'll be right back," he said. He returned carrying the worn velvet bag holding his *tefillin*. I will show you how to do this, just as my father showed me.

"Roll up the sleeve on your left arm. A Jew wears these straps on the head and on the weaker arm, as a reminder to grow stronger as a person. See how the box sits near your heart? To use your head in life is very important, but unless you balance the concerns of your heart and the logic in your head, your decisions can lack compassion.

"Slide the box on your head further down on your forehead. There. Hindus call that spot the third eye. It is very holy to have words of Torah there, between your eyes. *Tefillin* is a meditation; its purpose is to bring more love into the world."

"Daddy, why are you crying?"

"Because I never thought I'd ever do this again. Because I love you. And because teaching you, I remember my own father's love. And looking back, maybe some of the most important decisions I made as a leader during the war turned out to be good ones because of the good fortune of having grown up with Torah between my own eyes."

How to Put on Tefillin

Each step of *tefillin* practice has meaning. For example, by putting the *shel yad*, piece for the arm, on your weaker arm, the message is for this mitzvah to strengthen you. The root of *tefillin* (the Hebrew word *tefillin*) is tefillah, "prayer."

1. While standing, unwrap the *shel yad*'s coiled straps, leaving in place any knots or straps that have been slipped through a knot. Take off the decorative metal or cardboard box that protects the bayit.
2. Pull up your sleeve (or wear short sleeves), and open the leather loop wide so that you can slide your arm in and tighten the loop over your biceps.
3. Say the first blessing: *Baruch atah adonai eloheynu melech ha-olam asher kidshanu h'mitzvotav v'tzivanu l'hanee-ach tefillin* ("Blessed be . . . who guides us to holiness through doing mitzvot, by commanding the putting on of *tefillin*").
4. If you don't have a large bicep, it will help to wind above and below the box, on the flat edge beneath its box to hold it in place; otherwise you can end up with a bunch of coils around your wrist. Don't despair; it's normal for this to take lots of practice.
5. Now wrap seven times around your lower arm. Some communities have the custom of wrapping toward the body, others away. Each of the seven turns has a meaning; there are many interpretations. A powerful approach is to do each turn very slowly while focusing on one of the seven qualities the Jewish mystics teach are like a hologram of the Tree of Life happening inside of you and the Big Picture of the Universe as you do this. (If need be, you can focus on understanding these qualities and developing them in yourself with imaginary *tefillin*.) These seven qualities are the following:

Hessed: Unconditional loving-kindness
Gevurah: Strength and discipline
Tiferet: Compassion
Netzach: Endurance, ambition, drive
Hod: Extra attention to making something unique and beautiful

Yesod: Transmitting, sending something on that is ready
Malchut: Relaxing control of events; the joy of seeing what happens
    after you've given all you can

6. Now you can wind the rest of the leather strap around your palm. This is only temporary; you'll get back to this and do it again more elaborately in a minute.
7. Uncover the *shel rosh*, head piece, and put it over your head so that the box sits centered just below your hairline and then the knot will be behind your head above your neck. Let the two straps hang loosely on either side of your head and over your shoulders.
8. Recite the second blessing *baruch atah adonai eloheynu melech ha-olam asher kidshanu b'mitzvotav v'tzivanu al mitzvat tefillin* ("Blessed Be . . . guiding us to become holy through the mitzvah of *tefillin*." Many prayer books contain meditations to follow this point; one such asks God to "fill you with wisdom and to satisfy the desires of all living things."
9. With the seven windings in place on your arm, unwrap the length of strap around your palm and bring it over the top of your hand between your thumb and index finger down to the middle finger.
10. Wrap three times around the middle finger and then go back around your palm until you've used up the slack and can tuck the end in. Turn your hand over— surprise!—the configuration of the windings spells out one of the sacred names of God, *Shaddai*, "Nurturing One"—*Shin, Dalet, Yud*.
11. The blessing that is said now is the same one from the prophet Hosea that is said at a Jewish wedding, because *tefillin* is a commitment between a Jew and the Source of Life. Each of the seven windings is a weekday journey to prepare yourself for this moment. Over the years you can discover many possible interpretations for these Hebrew words.

V'eirastich li l'olam
I will be engaged with You forever
V'eirastich li b'tzedek
I will be engaged with You in justice

U'v'mish'pat
and deciding what's right
U'v'hessed
with loving-kindness
U'v'rachamim
and with compassion
v'eirastich li b'emunah
I will be engaged faithfully with You
v'yahdaht et YHVH.
So that you will know God.

What does the last verse mean? Some say, because there are no capital letters in Hebrew, that by emphasizing these qualities of living, we bring the experience of Godliness into the world. What do you think?

12. You can complete your *tefillin* meditation by sitting down and resting your head against the crook of the elbow of your wrapped arm. This will bring the *bayit* of the head *tefillin* near that of the arm, which will naturally be leaning up against your heart. Connecting head and heart through a mitzvah-centered life—that's the message!

A helpful photographic guide to laying *tefillin* can be accessed on the web at *tefillin.co.il*, and an on-line video guide by Rabbi Jay Spero is at jbuff.com/Tefvidrm.htm.

Tefillin are generally worn during morning prayers; afterward you can take your *tefillin* off or keep them on for a time of meditation or Torah study. When you take them off, first remove the strap around your fingers, then wind it around your palm; take off the *shel rosh*; wrap it up with its covering box back in place; wind its straps on it; put it away in the *tefillin* bag; then take off the rest of the *shel yad*, and wrap it up meditatively in its place in the bag too.

By the way, never wear *tefillin* to the bathroom—they have real sections of handwritten Torah inside. They're not only expensive; they can be damaged by moisture, extreme temperature, and misuse. If you're using an inherited set, check with a Judaica shop or a scribe to see if your *tefillin* need maintenance.

Tradition

The Holy One, Blessed Be, surrounded Israel with the commandment of *tefillin* for their heads, *tefillin* for their arms, *tzitzit* for their clothing and *mezuzot* for their doors.

—Talmud *Menachot* 43a-b

Michal the daughter of King Saul wore *tefillin* and the sages did not protest.

—Talmud *Eruvin* 96a

Tefillin take practice and support to become part of your life. Is there a morning service nearby where you will be comfortable and welcome? Or someone at home or in a B-Mitzvah class who can do this with you? If you are an adult B-Mitzvah, this is a wonderful practice to do simultaneously with a life partner or best friend.

You are not trapped into continuing these practices by sampling them. Many Jews are inconsistent in their practices, no matter how committed their intentions. We're people after all! If you begin some of the practices in this chapter and put them down at some point in your life, like the father of the young girl in the *tefillin* story, you will always have the effects of the practice deep within you. And it is always kosher to begin again.

We've covered a lot of ground in this chapter, from an overview of the structure of Jewish practice to the Torah ceremony, your role as a leader, your sacred name, and finally choosing and using personal ritual items. This is material for your season of preparation. If you've perused it in one reading, we've intentionally made sure that there's a lot to return to for study, day by day.

Now it's time to move on to the biggest step—becoming a witness, reader, and teacher of Torah on your B-Mitzvah day.

Chapter Five

Step-by-Step Guide to Giving a Great D'var Torah

On your *Bar/Bat Mitzvah* (B-Mitzvah) day, the power of the pulpit will be handed over to you. You will have the responsibility of helping your community to find meaning for living from within the *parsha*, the Torah portion for the week. Giving over meaningful guidance on the Torah portion during a religious service is not so much a speech as it is a mitzvah, a sacred act called "giving a *d'var Torah*." A *d'var*, "a word," of Torah, is a brief teaching where you connect your Torah portion with the heart, mind, and spirit of those present. Israelis often refer to this practice as a *derasha* or *drash*, an "explanation" of the Torah portion.

Although a Torah teaching is often an oral presentation, yours can take many forms. Whether you can offer a self-crafted talk, play, satire, ballad, dance, visual art, poetry, or other format will depend upon local norms, the flexibility of your setting, and your own talents. This is a precious opportunity that is meant to reflect who you are as a member of the *minyan* of your life and to relate those ideals, concerns, and ideas that you believe will be meaningful to those in attendance.

You are not meant to be alone in the task of crafting your Torah teaching. Nor is someone else to create it for you. Some will believe it is a gift to do this for you, so decline and thank them for caring so deeply. You will find interesting examples of *divrei Torah* in this book and on the Internet, but think of these as springboards for finding your own unique approach. Every person has the ability to accomplish this phase of the initiation process with integrity. Let those who seek to help you know that you want yours to be an original work, so that you will experience the full benefit of the B-Mitzvah as a ritual of initiation.

Why Give A D'var Torah?

First, you might rightfully ask: Why is such a major task being asked of you? Surely enough insightful commentary has already been written in every generation! Nevertheless, to each generation passes the opportunity to make something more of this world; your visions, views, values, and voices matter. Your people want to hear your voice, to know you are learning our sacred texts and traditions and that you are able to bring us important and new ideas based on your studies and perspective. Your presence in the process is very important, because into your hands is being given the opportunity to shape the future by passing the light of Torah through the lens of changing times.

Is it surprising to learn that Judaism values change? Although our tradition can look formidable and permanent, this has never been the case. In the Talmud, Torah is compared to water, as an "ever flowing stream." The nature of a stream is to change according to the terrain it encounters: the more rocks—the more rapids, like life. Jewish people do not relate to the Torah as fundamentalists who expect rock solid, immutable answers. We understand it to be a stream, a living source of inspiration for all the times in which we will live.

Strategies for understanding and practicing our faith were often different in the past and have evolved dramatically over time. When we look back in Jewish time, many examples of major change become visible. Notice that "current" is a water metaphor: when you're busy coping with a strong current in your life, it's hard to remember that strategies were often different in times past and may need to adapt for times to come. Here are some examples of major changes in Jewish practices over time.

- According to the literal meaning of Torah, a rebellious teenager is supposed to be stoned to death; you don't see anyone doing that these days!
- Jacob the patriarch and kings such as David long engaged in having multiple simultaneous wives (polygamy), a practice that Ashkenazi Jews officially discontinued only about a thousand years ago.
- Abraham and Sarah served milk and meat together to their guests; those who keep kosher today don't.
- We used to sacrifice animals and burn their fat and entrails to communicate with God; when the temple was destroyed, we were able to discover the greater power of words and deeds to make a better world.

There are a great many more examples of change in Judaism. For centuries it's been our responsibility to read and reread our sacred documents, to understand what they mean, and to reinterpret how they can apply to our lives today. For example, B-Mitzvah students will often chant and interpret the prophetic writings known as *Haftorah*. This body of sacred literature is filled with depictions of urgent ethical problems in Jewish life that led the prophets to call passionately for change—in the community, in leaders, and sometimes in the way people of their times were practicing Judaism.

You are a precious member of our people. Your life is the lens you will bring to Torah. We need to hear your vision of what is important for us to pay attention to in the Torah and *Haftorah* portions. You are invited to step up to the plate as a leader and teacher for the Jewish and human future.

That said, the service is not about the B-Mitzvah student; it is about ensuring a meaningful experience of prayer, receiving Torah, and the celebration of Shabbat. Taking on a role of leadership in a service involves *shiflut*, "humility"; one serves without requiring a spotlight. Gratitude to teachers and family and the family and community's *nachas*, "pride," at the accomplishment of a B-Mitzvah initiate are important and must receive serious air time. But these are often best expressed at the reception or after the religious ceremonies have concluded and before announcements. Many communities have one or more B'nei Mitzvah (the plural of the term) on every weekend, and the experience of Shabbat and the special traditions of the congregation can get lost if the B'nei Mitzvah and their many visiting family members are allowed to predominate.

We will discuss matters of expressing pride and appreciation, including the giving and receiving of gifts, in our final chapter. What follows in this chapter are some ideas and guidelines on how to make your Torah teaching original, meaningful, and expressive of your unique identity and concerns.

Finding Your Torah Portion

The Torah, also known in book form as the *Chumash* (pronounced khuh-mahsh), means "Five," as in the Five Books of Moses. The Torah is

Tip

Advice for the Torah Portion
Always check carefully for what Torah portion is assigned to a given date.

Hebcal.com is an easy place to look up which Torah and *Haftorah* (prophetic) portions are matched with any given Shabbat in the year.

On occasion two Torah portions will be assigned to one Shabbat in order to fit the full sequence of readings into a given year.

Holidays have special portions assigned, not simply the next portion in the sequence.

Traditionally, there are certain blackout dates during which Jewish life-cycle events are prohibited due to their proximity to other sacred occasions. Check Bmitzvah.org for these specifics.

THE FIFTY-FOUR PORTIONS OF TORAH

Name	Book	Verses	Name	Book	Verses
	Genesis		Metzora		14:1-15:33
Bereshit		1:1-6:8	Acharei—Mot		16:1-18:30
Noach		6:9-11:32	Kedoshim		19:1-20:27
Lech-Lecha		12:1-17:27	Emor		21:1-24:23
Vayera		18:1-22:24	Behar		25:1-26:2
Hayyei-Sarah		23:1-25:18	Bechukotai		26:3-27:34
Toldot		25:19-28:9		Numbers	
Vayetze		28:10-32:3	Bamidbar		1:1-4:20
Vayishlach		32:4-36:43	Naso		4:21-7:89
Vayeshev		37:1-40:23	Behaalotcha		8:1-12:16
Miketz		41:1-44:17	Shelach-Lecha		13:1-15:41
Vayigash		44:18-47:27	Korach		16:1-18:32
Vayechi		47:28-50:26	Chukat		19:1-22:1
	Exodus		Balak		22:2-25:9
Shemot		1:1—6:1	Pinchas		25:10-30:1
Vaera		6:2-9:35	Matot		30:2-32:42
Bo		10:1-13:16	Masei		33:1-36:13
Beshalach		13:17-17:16		Deuteronomy	
Yitro		18:1-20:23	Devarim		1:1-3:22
Mishpatim		21:1-24:18	Vaetchanan		3:23-7:11
Teruma		25:1-27:19	Ekev		7:12-11:25
Tetzave		27:20-30:10	Re'eh		11:26-16:17
Ki-Tisa		30:11-34:35	Shoftim		16:18-21:9
Vayakhel		35:1-38:20	Kiteitze		21:10-25:19
Pekudei		38:21-40:38	Ki Tavo		26:1-29:8
	Leviticus		Nitzavim		29:9-30:20
Vayikra		1:1-5:26	Vayelech		31:1-31:30
Tzav		6:1-8:36	Ha-azinu		32:1-52
Shemini		9:1-11:47	Vezot Habracha		33:1-34:12
Tazria		12:1-13:59			

studied and chanted aloud in weekly segments known as the *parsha*, or "portion." This annual process ends and starts all over again on the holy day known as Simchat Torah, which is a day of "rejoicing in the Torah." Because Judaism follows a lunar cycle, with certain years containing leap months, one year's Jewish calendar does not often help with the next. For the same reason, in some years a single date will have two portions. On festivals and holidays, special portions are read that go out of order with the sequence of the year.

Every *parsha* has a particular name derived from an early word or phrase in its verses. For example the first portion is named after its first word, *Bereshit*, "In the beginning." The accompanying table lists all the Torah portions in order.

Your *Haftorah* portion will be drawn from the post-Biblical period Jewish sacred texts known as Neviim, Prophets. These are found in the TaNaKh, the full canon of the Jewish Bible. The TaNaKh contains three sections: the Torah (Five Books of Moses); the Neviim (Joshua, Judges, Kings, and prophets Isaiah, Jeremiah, Ezekiel, Hosea, Joel, Amos, Micah, Habakkuk, Zechariah, and Malachi), and the Ketuvim (Psalms, Proverbs, Job, Song of Songs, Book of Ruth, Lamentations, Ecclesiastes, Esther, Daniel, Ezra-Nechemiah, and Chronicles).

Formatting Your D'var Torah

The possibilities for creativity in giving a *d'var Torah* are virtually limitless and must be guided by a student's talents, interests, life experience, and personal challenges. Just as we saw in an earlier chapter how Ben crafted a ballad about the experience of the brothers as the *d'var Torah* for his *parsha*, his twin sister, Sara, ultimately composed, choreographed, and performed an interpretive dance; other approaches might include the following:

- Composing a play and organizing friends to help perform it
- Composing and playing a piece of music
- Shooting and editing a short film to express your *d'var*

- Sculpting, weaving, painting, or making a collage about a powerful moment in the text

If you make a film, this could be shown after Shabbat during the reception in communities that don't use media on Shabbat.

Creative expressions are important interpretive options for B-Mitzvah students with disabilities. A deaf person can sign and have an interpreter. An autistic B-Mitzvah student created a handmade doll for each character in the story of Joseph and the many-colored coat. His older sister chanted his *d'var Torah* while he enacted the story with the dolls, without talking, through movement. Because leading prayer was unrealistic for him, he also created a *siddur*, a prayer book with his own original drawings for each of the major prayers in the Shabbat morning service.

Are there limits to the applications of creativity in giving a *d'var Torah*? Yes, matters of good taste, ethical speech, and sensitivity to the diversity of those who will be learning with you are very important. This is not a time to express prejudice toward any group, nor is it time to cause dissension in your community by taking a political position. You are teaching at a service; your task is to alert, educate, enliven, inspire.

Can you point out injustices? Absolutely, it is incumbent upon a student of Torah to do so. The fine line you walk is in how to point out the injustice without humiliating anyone or advocating a particular political party or partisan perspective. Shabbat is for peace, not politics. It will be up to people of conscience who learn from you to take action in all places where justice can be advanced.

Getting Acquainted With Your Torah Portion

Regardless of the format you will use to teach about the *parska* at your B-Mitzvah, you will need methods to extract meaning from your Torah portion. The sequence that follows will help with your empowerment, to ensure that your vision, voice, views, and values are able to enter the dialogue of the generations that create an ever-living Torah for our people.

First Reading

Begin by reading through your portion in one to three sittings to get a quick overview of plot, characters, scenes, and themes. Reading out loud tends to help because the Torah often contains a great deal of dialogue, action, and emotion.

A *parsha* can contain many elements, such as:

- Dramatic stories
- Guidelines, commandments, and laws
- Architectural and decorative instructions
- Military battles
- Songs
- Scenes of the sacrificial system
- Encounters with God

The Five Books of Moses, the Torah, cover different periods of time in the development of the Jewish people as a civilization.

Approximate Time Covered	Book of Bible	Hebrew Name
2300 years	Genesis	Bereshit
210 years	Exodus	Shemot
30 years	Leviticus	Vayikra
38 years	Numbers	Bamidbar
27 days	Deuteronomy	Devarim

Your Next Step

Reread your portion, gradually, over several sessions. Read it in Hebrew if you can readily understand it, or in a translation in the language in which you are most comfortable.

A *d'var* Torah means a word or matter of Torah. So fear not; you do not have to teach on every aspect of your Torah portion on the day of your B-Mitzvah. At the beginning of your B-Mitzvah preparation process, your task is to study the entire *parsha* for your own sake. You will need resources and mentors to help you explore the portion from structural, intellectual, emotional, and spiritual vantage points. Lots of interesting ideas will begin to emerge during this process.

At your B-mitzvah, through your *d'var* you will show your depth of study, skill at verbal and intellectual analysis of the text, and growing emotional maturity. It is your task to go beyond what the portion means to you, into the realm of empathy for those in attendance. This means your task will be to highlight opportunities for others to experience meaning for living through this portion. This will require that you become selective and focus on specific points in the portion.

The Outline

Create an outline of your *parsha*, so that the flow of precisely what is happening becomes clear to you. Many of us learned folk versions of Bible stories in the early years of religious school or got our impression of what the text is from Disney animations or Hollywood renditions of major stories like the Ten Commandments, but these versions are all interpretations and tend to differ significantly from the actual words of the Torah. The original may prove to be a surprising and more interesting read for you!

Young adult B-Mitzvah students may not have been introduced to the idea of an outline in school yet. This is a very useful educational tool that students of all ages will want to know. Creating both detailed and short outlines will help to focus your mind and clarify the text for you. Many different Torah portions will be featured in this chapter along with many different approaches to formulating your *d'var Torah*. Let's start with a short outline of *Hayyei Sarah*, the life of Sarah (Genesis 23:1-25:18):

I.   Sarah dies and is buried.
   A. Sarah dies.
   B. Abraham goes to where she died and grieves for her.
   C. He enters negotiations with the locals to buy a burial site for her.

D. Abraham obtains the site and the field it borders.

E. He buries her there, in the Cave of Machpelah.

II. Abraham's servant fulfills an assignment to find a wife for Isaac.

    A. Abraham asks a senior servant to take the assignment of finding a wife for Isaac from among Abraham's family in the city of Nahor.

    B. The servant departs and asks God for a sign of the right girl, which he decides would be one who draws water for him and his camels.

    C. The sign is indeed fulfilled by a girl from Abraham's kin, Rebecca.

    D. The servant explains his reason for coming, of the amazing confirmation of the sign, and asks for permission to bring Rebecca to Isaac.

    E. The family wants time with Rebecca before she leaves.

    F. The servant is determined to depart the next day.

    G. The family asks her opinion, and Rebecca says: "I will go."

    H. The family holds a blessing ceremony and sends them on their journey.

III. Isaac and Rebecca meet and marry.

    A. The servant guides Rebecca to a field where Isaac is meditating.

    B. He looks up and sees camels approaching.

    C. She sees Isaac and falls off her camel.

    D. She finds out who he is.

    E. The servant briefs Isaac on who she is.

    F. Isaac takes her to his (deceased) mother's tent, and they are married.

    G. Isaac loves her and is consoled for the loss of his mother (Sarah).

IV. Abraham remarries.

    A. His wife's name is Keturah.

    B. Together they have six children and from them eleven grandchildren.

    C. Still, Abraham's estate goes to Isaac.

    D. Abraham sends all his children by concubines away with gifts.

    E. Abraham dies at 175 biblical years of age.

    F. Isaac and Ishmael bury him in the cave with Sarah.

V. The genealogy of Ishmael is given.
  A. Ishmael has twelve sons.
  B. All are princes with territory and towns.
  C. Ishmael dies at 137 biblical years.
  D. His sons go on to dominate their region.

Did the outline hold any surprises for you? Such surprises are a good place to start looking for a basis for your *d'var Torah*.

Finding Meaning In Your Torah Portion

The most interesting meanings to be found in your Torah portion will not tend to be obvious. That is part of the genius of the Torah's design. It is constructed in such a way as to afford apparently infinite possibilities for finding new meanings in its stories, characters, symbols, commandments, and practices. Exploring your Torah portion can be a lot of fascinating fun; it is a prism filled with doorways to higher consciousness.

It helps to begin with a wide, open-hearted curiosity about your portion. As time goes on, you will need to narrow your focus onto the moments, key words, phrases, commands, tradition, and questions about your *parsha* that most capture your spirit and that might be meaningful to those who will be at your B-Mitzvah.

Torah Portion as a Script

Consider your portion as though it is a script for a screenplay. This can help matters come to life. After filling in the elements in each of the categories that follow, create a sketch of the backdrop, props, and characters for each scene:

Location(s): Where does the story take place—desert, forest, sea?
Characters: Describe them, name their qualities, even imagine their
  looks and manner.

Symbols and props: What symbols are involved? What props might the
   screenplay need—water, stone tablets, swords, or frogs?
Major events: What events take place—battle, love scene, sacrifice?

You have been dealing with the *p'shat* of the text, the "simple" or
basic story line. Let's move on.

The Significance of Translations

By definition all translations are interpretations, often reflecting specific
ideological orientations. If you take a shelf full of different translations
of the Torah and open them all to the same chapter and verse, often
you will find significant variations in the meaning that the translator
assigned.

For example, in the *parsha* titled Vayera in Genesis 22:2, some
translations have God saying to Abraham, "Take your son" (and sacrifice
him). Others render it as a request and not a command: "Please take
your son," which is more faithful to the meaning of the Hebrew. What a
difference to the story if this is viewed as a request or a command!

Hebrew is a language perfect for spirituality because words have
many shades of meaning; this allows the translation of a verse to depend
on the current situation of the reader. Those who translate the Bible
have their own needs and biases. So unless you are fairly skillful in
Hebrew, look at more than one translation.

If you are very new to Hebrew literacy, a good mentor will be
able to show you even a few of the portals of higher meaning that are
encoded within the Hebrew. It is here that you are likely to discover the
excitement so many feel about Torah study.

For example, in the section we first outlined in this chapter, Genesis
24:64, how did Rebecca react when she first saw Isaac: *Va-tee-pol min ha-
gamal.* She fell off the camel!

Have you ever been so surprised or excited by someone that
one could say you "fell off your camel" for him or her? Try having a
conversation with family, mentors, and friends about the difference
between falling in love and growing in love. See how only a few words
can trigger a great awareness that can form the basis for a heartfelt *d'var
Torah*. This is the power of the Torah to deepen our lives by making

room for each other's wisdom to emerge.

But this dramatic moment of interpretive opportunity is often unavailable in translations of the Bible published before the year 2000. It has taken a long time for women to be read as realistic characters. Prior translators could only imagine presenting our matriarch-to-be like a lady, and so you would find them saying that she "descended from her camel" or "alighted."

Translators have conscious and unconscious agendas having to do with when they lived, how they grew up, what their approach to Jewish observance was, and more. Christian scholars who have translated the Torah are also reading events through their own Christian-values lens, which is different from viewing events through a Jewish-values lens.

Select those edition(s) of the Torah from which you will study with great consciousness. Translators have a huge impact on what the text can mean. It is helpful to own more than one publication of the Torah or TaNaCH, so that you can compare the translators' perspectives and begin to find your own.

Your Reactions

Does any aspect of the *parsha* arouse your passion? Does something seem unfair, exciting, frightening, peculiar, missing, or momentous? Trust your gut. Places in your portion that arouse strong feelings in you are where you, personally, will be best able to mine for meaning.

Here's an example of a *d'var Torah* based on a passionate awareness. It is for the *parsha* known as *Chukat* (pronounced khu-kaht, there's no "ch" sound in Hebrew) (Numbers 19:1-22:1):

> In my Torah portion, Moses and Aaron learn they will not enter the promised land because instead of listening precisely to God's instructions for finding water, Moses hits a rock instead of speaking to it. It is amazing to see that Moses disobeys God. How could this be?
>
> By looking back just before this portion, I discovered that Moses' and Aaron's sister Miriam has just died. She not only arranged for the princess to find baby Moses in the water, she also had a talent for finding water and leading the people in dance and song. Lively Miriam helped the people survive in the wilderness

through her special talents. Now that she is gone, they have to figure out how to go on without her.

I've noticed that people do strange things when they are very sad; sometimes they get angry with God. That's how I felt when a classmate died of leukemia; I was very angry with God. I'm older now, and my ways of thinking have changed; now I pray for the courage to dedicate my life to working for a cure, and I believe that acts of nature aren't personal.

But in the Torah, why doesn't Moses get understanding for his anger from God? Surely what he did can be forgiven when you think of the circumstances.

I think it's because he wasn't able to control himself in front of the people. Leaders have such a strong sense of responsibility that they might think they can't take a day off. But leaders need to be able to prepare someone else to lead long in advance of when a problem arises. Then when something devastating happens in their personal lives, people don't have to worry that they will try to function when it is not humanly possible.

Leaders are only human, and I believe this story about Moses is to teach about the importance of knowing when you are fit to lead, to go to work, to parent, or even to captain a school team, and when not. It seems to me this applies today, at home, and in the government.

Let's all try to learn from Moses' mistake. I have three blessings to give today:

The first is for all the leaders in the room to have the wisdom to know when not to go to work. Sometimes the work you need to do is at home and inside yourself.

My second blessing is for all of us to do what we can to eat and exercise and support ourselves to live in good health.

My third blessing is also for all of us. In the course of life, we will all lose someone to a terrible disease. Judaism teaches that we are partners with God in creation. May we all be blessed to have the ability to actively support medical research. Thank you.

This *d'var Torah* used the *p'shat* of the story, the simple facts, to support important emotional insights about major challenges we all face in life. This is one effective way to approach creating a *d'var Torah*.

Characteristics of a Memorable B-Mitzvah D'var Torah
A memorable B-Mitzvah *d'var Torah*

- Helps those present to connect some aspect(s) of the Torah portion to their own lives
- Touches on something in your life that is likely to have happened in the lives of others in the room
- Offers emotional honesty; is very real
- Takes an ancient event and interprets it in the light of current affairs
- Directly addresses those present to involve and empower them—using "I," "you," and "we" language and ideas
- Highlights ethical principles and action opportunities that most of those present can realistically implement
- Brings an aspect of Jewish practice to life, a mitzvah, a blessing, a holiday ritual, a sacred phrase, and so on
- Uses guidance from commentaries of the sages
- Adds new perspectives from our own time
- Reflects the human capacity for constructive change
- Offers hope, insight, and inspiration for living

Reflect upon the *d'var Torah* you have just read by taking a highlighter and seeing if each of the points in this list is represented in it. Notice your own reactions, and make notes about what you would improve or change to make this *d'var Torah* more meaningful to you or those who you expect will be learning Torah from you at your B-Mitzvah.

Let's continue with ways to study your portion that will help you learn from it and prepare to teach from it to others.

Characters and Objects
As a way to focus in, prepare a resume for a character in your *parsha*. This will involve reading other chapters to learn more about this person. Take Moses, for example. What would have been on his resume? Experienced slave? No, he trained in the palace of the pharaoh. You might try writing his resume; there is a lot to discover.

If there are characters or objects in your portion, think of one question you might ask each of them and write it to them as a short letter. Here is an example for an object:

Dear Broken Tablets:
    Moses sat in the cleft of a rock and came down with you. Was the rock originally whole, and were you created from it? How did it feel to be chosen to have the Ten Commandments engraved upon you? What was it like being dashed to the ground when Moses saw everyone worshiping a golden calf?
    I hope to find an answer from you arising in my thoughts and dreams.

Thanks!
—Dana

Now imagine you are this character or object, and write a letter answering the questions you've posed.

To harvest lots of insights, after writing your own response, show your letter of inquiry to others whose opinions you value and who are willing to read your Torah portion. Enjoy their answers; discuss them without putting anyone down for having different reactions than you do. Torah looks very different through the lens of each person's life. There's no right answer, just many personal answers. Perhaps in your *d'var Torah* you will share some of the responses you gather from the *minyan* of your life.

Focus on Characters and Parallels to Current Events

Another way to bring the *parsha* to life is to focus in on characters and parallels to current events. For example, aspects of the life of Joshua appear in several Torah portions.

Tip

Seek out a Regular Study Buddy

A basic principle in Judaism is that Torah study is not a solitary practice. Listening only to yourself as a source for meaning really limits the possibilities, compared to studying in a group or with a friend or mentor. In fact, the compilation of aphorisms of our sages, Pirke Avot 1:6a, says that when you are ready to begin your Jewish learning: "Acquire a teacher, take a friend for yourself." A study buddy is known in our tradition as a *hevruta*, or "friendship" partner. You will be surprised how time flies during *hevruta* study and how multiple fascinating meanings for your portion will emerge.

Who could your B-Mitzvah study buddy be? A tutor, parent, sibling? Another B-Mitzvah student? A grandparent, aunt, or uncle? Your rabbi or cantor? Someone who shares a talent with you—a musician, artist, actor, author?

Each time you meet with your study buddy, take a few minutes to read a few verses of your portion aloud. Notice each word in a sentence and take time to wonder about the meaning of words, terms, decisions, ideas, the plot, everything. Keep notes about ideas that jump out at you as important. Share about how you and your buddy have confronted issues or experiences in your lives like those in your text. Let the Torah portion connect you to each other through your feelings, thoughts, and questions.

Meaning Makers

Congregations could do a great mitzvah for B-Mitzvah students by organizing corps of meaning makers, volunteer *d'var Torah* study buddies of various ages, skills, and talents. The person who has the skills to teach trope, the notes for chanting the Torah portion, will not always have the training or time to help with your search for meaning. Students who have meaning-making study buddies often report these as turning into particularly important mentoring relationships that can last long into the future.

In *parshat Ki-Tissa* we learn that Joshua was Moses' valet and stayed in the tent with Moses every time he came back down from his vision quests on the mountain top.

Later, in *parshat Shelach-Lecha*, Joshua serves as one of the twelve spies who go ahead of the Israelites to check out the promised land. Only two of the twelve return with a positive report, Joshua and Caleb. Only they survive the wilderness time to enter the holy land.

Ultimately, Joshua, in *parshat Pinchas*, inherits the mantle of leadership from Moses by way of *smichah*, a ritual laying-on of hands. This ritual of transmission of leadership is still used to ordain rabbis at most seminaries.

Joshua will go on to fight the battle of Jericho, after sending two (not twelve, one from each tribe, as Moses had in *Shelach-Lecha*) handpicked spies to check out Jericho. This spy story in Joshua 2:1-24 is in fact the *Haftorah* for *parshat Shelach-Lecha*.

Rabbinic commentaries and *midrashim* stress the strategic importance of Moses having chosen one spy from each tribe. Because the early Israelites were unaccustomed to battle, the sages suggest, Moses hoped the selection of representatives from each tribe would help to get everyone motivated.

These portions are pregnant with so many *d'var Torah* opportunities!

Even with only two positive reports brought back, Moses forges forward. How is this similar to the behavior of modern leaders in pursuing goals they believe essential over the protests or apathy of the citizenry? Is this happening around you? You can highlight the importance of watching how leaders manipulate the media to secure their own ends. What do you think? How do your guests want to learn about the facts on the ground regarding key issues? Who gets appointed to leadership? Why did Joshua cut back to two instead of twelve spies? What did he learn from observing the challenges that beset Moses? What did young Joshua think about or talk about when he was with Moses at those times?

What was their relationship like? What is it like to be a young aide-de-camp for a famous person? What is the difference between mentoring and exploitation? This line of thinking might lead into a *d'var Torah* on an issue that often appears in current events: scandals in government when an official has been sexually inappropriate with support staff or used others as "fall guys" for their own mistakes. Such a *d'var Torah* might include criteria you believe important for ethical and effective leadership training and the role of leaders as mentors.

Symbols and Metaphors

Words in the Torah sometimes mean far more than meets the eye; they also can serve as symbols and metaphors. This is a third dimension of Torah study, known as *remez*, "hint." A symbol is an object that carries meaning beyond its everyday sense. For example, the Star of David is a symbol worn to show that one is proud to be Jewish. A candle flame is a metaphor for the soul in Judaism, so when someone dies Jews light a candle as a memorial that symbolizes the light that person's soul brought into our lives.

Identifying metaphors in the text can open up all sorts of new possibilities for understanding a Torah portion. A concordance is a tool that lists every word in the Torah and all the verses in which it occurs. Scholars determine the meaning of each word by comparing occurrences. Concordances are available on-line and as books. Objects that appear frequently are often metaphors, and their meaning in one context will enrich their meaning in another place in the Torah. For example, in Judaism water is a metaphor for God as presence, abundance, and flow. Rock is a metaphor for God as a solid, just, dependable source of life and support in both the Torah and the *siddur*, or "prayer book." For example:

- In the famous biblical dream known as Jacob's Ladder, Jacob uses a rock for his pillow.
- Moses has a rock placed beneath him when he tires of holding his arms aloft during a key battle scene.
- Moses hits the rock in anger when the people need water.

- Moses sits in the cleft of the rock to receive the Ten Commandments.
- The prayer *Adon Olam* calls God the "Rock that anchors me in times of distress."
- Psalm 92 calls God "My Rock, in which nothing appears bent."
- And of course, there's the Hanukkah hymn "Rock of Ages—*Maoz Tzur.*"

So how does knowing that rock is a metaphor for God add meaning to a *parsha?* Here's a brief *d'var Torah* that draws on this metaphor:

In my Torah portion, Jacob is a young man. When he spends a night alone out in the wilderness on the way to finding a mate, Jacob uses a rock for a pillow.

A rock for a pillow. This sounds similar to the fable of the pea under the princess's mattress. Torah was originally transmitted orally and is full of sacred stories. Can you imagine sitting around listening to this story and having the image of Jacob selecting a rock and putting his head on it like a pillow? Why a rock? What could it stand for?

On the one hand, the rock could be a metaphor for the rockiness in his life. He has just stolen his brother's birthright and is fleeing a difficult scene. His family encourages his departure with the suggestion that this is a fitting time to journey to his mother's side of the family in search of a mate.

What an exciting, uncomfortable, even scary time for Jacob! The anxiety and ethical problems of teaming up with his mother to trick his father and brother were important subjects of last week's *divrei Torah* [plural]. Today we must keep that aspect in mind, along with the trauma of his needing to flee; there is the excitement of anticipating finding a mate and now the danger of sleeping out in the wilderness all alone.

What a night for Jacob! I imagine many thoughts were churning in his head. Perhaps the recent incidents were replaying themselves; emotions like guilt and fear must have plagued him. This chapter of his life is very much like having a rock for a pillow! It must have been harder for him to sleep than it is for me on the night before school starts each year.

Still the body can't go on without sleep. So sleep Jacob does; and what's more, he dreams.

In his dream a ladder grows up all the way to heaven where angelic messengers bring Jacob a prediction that his future will be quite wonderful, complete with details. He interprets this sweet dream as a message from God. He exclaims that God was in this place, and he had not previously known it. The rock was like a seed that grew his dream and vision of a bright future. The rock symbolizes the presence of God in this story. Jacob realizes he was never really alone. He commemorates the site as sacred by setting up the rock as a monument.

From this story of Jacob, we also can learn the importance of listening to our dreams. It may feel at times as if life has given you a rock for a pillow. Take that rock and let it be a seed for you too. It is not very helpful to keep listening to your own churning thoughts. Listening for something new is a very important idea in Judaism.

In every mezuzah there is a prayer called the *Shema*, "listen." Perhaps Jacob's dream tells us why Jews say the *Shema* before going to sleep. Could it be that saying the *Shema* is like putting up a mezuzah on the doorpost to our dreams?

Tonight when you go home to bed after having a great time at my *Bat Mitzvah* party, you might try saying the *Shema* and listening for the voice of God in your dreams. Listen for something new and see what comes. I bless you to have *chalomot paz*, as is said in Hebrew, "golden dreams."

Thank you.

Again, go through the *d'var Torah* you have just read and highlight it in relationship to the list of memorable *d'var Torah* points. Ask yourself how it could be improved to speak better to you and those you expect at your B-Mitzvah. Notice that this material doesn't have to be given as a talk. The insights from this *parsha* could serve as the impetus to create a dramatic skit as the form of *d'var Torah* to be given, perhaps of a reporter doing an inside story on Jacob's life and what happened to him out there that night.

Create Your Own Bibliodrama

Midrash is a *d'var Torah* form in which you imagine possible scenarios out of unspoken moments on the part of characters in your Torah portion. This is not at all a heretical thing to do; making *midrash* is an ancient Jewish practice of sages and Torah students of all ages. Our sages have written multiple *midrashim* on every Torah portion, and they reveal Jewish life and values viewed through the eyes of Jewish men. Volumes of commentary and *midrashim* [plural of the term] by Jewish women began being published for the first time in Jewish history in the twentieth century. Although you will likely often be inspired and sometimes troubled by the *midrashim* of others, making your own is powerful, perfectly legitimate, and lots of fun. Your own *midrash* can become a *d'var Torah* in the form of a story, a play, dance, painting, and much more.

Here is an example of a *midrash*-style *d'var Torah:*

In this week's Torah portion, *parshat* Vayeitzi, Rachel and Leah leave their ancestral home with their husband, Jacob, to set up an independent household. The biblical tales of these sisters are troubling to me. Rachel and Jacob fell in love; he works seven years to marry her; her father substitutes her older sister during the wedding ceremony, and it takes another seven years for him to add his beloved Rachel as his wife.

There must be so much going on between the lines in this Torah portion. In the process called making *midrash*, one looks for missing dialogue opportunities in the Torah. This portion has so many missing scenarios that we could make a whole movie!

• Where was Rachel and Leah's mother when all this was going on? Didn't she have something to say about this situation? Or is she deceased?

- Or did Rachel and Leah each have different mothers? Just like the twelve tribes will have different mothers, Rachel, Leah, Bilhah, and Zilpah.
- Why is there not one mother-daughter dialogue in the whole Torah?
- How did Rachel feel when she was cheated out of being a bride and had to wait seven years for the touch of her beloved? Who did she talk to about it?
- What was it like for Rachel to have to wait seven years for the chance to have children in a culture where this defined your worth to the tribe? Wasn't she an old maid by biblical standards by the time she was able to marry?
- This was before antibiotics, when people often died from infection and when plagues could decimate populations. Rachel couldn't assume she'd survive to become a bride. What was it like to be her?
- Leah had many children with Jacob before Rachel and he married or conceived. What kind of aunt did Rachel prove to be?
- How did Jacob repress his feelings toward Laban?
- How did he manage to be with Leah and yet see Rachel around every day?
- Was Laban an abusive father? Why didn't his daughters demand a different outcome? There is a Torah portion about the daughters of Zelophehad where they stand up for their inheritance rights and are granted them. Why didn't Rachel rebel, run away, or confront her father? Why did Leah agree to stand in and marry Jacob first?

We already know through a back door how Leah and Jacob felt. When Leah names her sons, she incorporates her feelings into their naming ritual:

Leah calls her firstborn Reuben because "the Lord has seen (Hebrew: *ra'ah*) my affliction" and "now my husband will love me (*yeh'eh-hah-vah-ni*)" (Genesis 29:32). Her second son she names Shimon because "G-d heard that I was hated, and so gave me also this [one]" (*Shim-on* literally means "He hears affliction," Genesis 29:33). Her third she hopefully calls Levi, saying "this time my husband will become attached (*yillaweh*) to me" (Genesis 29:34).

What a sad situation. Imagine being the child of such a household. And indeed, Reuben goes on to make a major ethical mistake in his life by sleeping with his father's concubine Bilhah, the mother of two of the tribes, Dan and Naftali. Jacob's sons will later kill their sister Dina's husband, Shechem, who converted to be with her. She gets no voice of her own in the Torah either. We have to find women's words in the Torah through back doors and in the white space between the letters.

It is actually a wonder that I am standing here before you as a *Bat Mitzvah*! This is such a new phenomenon for our people, introduced in the twentieth century. Matters of gender and justice have begun to concern me greatly, and I hope they are important to you too. Can you imagine: a key rabbinical council of the state of Israel disbanded last year rather than allow women rabbis to sit on it! I hope you will speak up when you see these forms of injustice.

In some movements women still can't lead services or sign religious documents or sit on councils to make rabbinic decisions. In some parts of the spectrum, women who are abandoned by their husbands or who leave abusive husbands that won't give them a religious divorce can never remarry in a religious Jewish context. They are called *agunot*, "chained women." How can any kind of Jew perpetuate this? Why would any rabbi want to do so? Sometimes these women are blackmailed by their husbands to get a religious divorce. Why have religious courts not struck down this practice? I know that Judaism can be changed. We don't have polygamy any more, nor do we stone rebellious children, which is what the Torah says we should do. What is going on here?

Let's look closer to home. Attending this service are Jews who sit on community boards and who vote on allocations for major Jewish organizations. Are there criteria about justice for women that influence the funding patterns of these organizations? And where such criteria exist, are they followed? I saw in the Jewish newspaper a headline that few heads of major Jewish organizations are women; such posts are most often given to males. Women in executive jobs in the Jewish community have been widely found to be receiving less pay. Do you act to create job parity and equity for Jewish women wherever and whenever you can?

This is the first century in which Jewish women have access to high-level study of sacred texts in yeshivot and universities. We are being trained to join our brothers in leadership. When will all women be sought out for leadership and scholarship roles and be treated fairly in them?

I have discovered that this matter is in all our hands. Did you know that the principal of our Hebrew school was being paid less than her male predecessor and working longer hours with more duties? As my mitzvah project, I got all the students and parents to sign a petition of protest, and the board rapidly agreed to correct the situation.

I bless everyone here to have the courage to speak up, to take Jewish women out of the margins and onto the heart of the page of Jewish history as it is being written every day.

Look at the news photos of world leaders and see if we are visible in any significant number. We are not. Many studies show that women have more relational, collaborative ways of thinking. I ask you: Can a peace process afford to have 50 percent of humanity be absent? I value the vision, views, and values of Jewish men no more or less than those of Jewish women.

The New York Times recently reported a study showing that marriages with sons last longer than couples who have only female children. It is time for humanity to value daughters equally! I look forward to hearing your thoughts about effective action after services. Thank you.

Welcome Powerful Moments of Awareness

Sometimes when you are studying Torah, especially with a *hevruta* partner, a powerful awareness will slip out as though it was hidden in the text waiting for you to be born so that it could become known in your generation. This is the fourth level of study, known as *sod* (pronounced sohd) "secret." Hidden meanings can emerge in any of the many Torah study methods. You cannot force the *sod* of Torah to come; it just sometimes does, and you will recognize the feeling of a *sod* moment immediately. It feels like awe.

At Camp Emanuel in the Berkshires, a group of elders and B-Mitzvah students were studying Torah together using the *midrash*-making technique called bibliodrama. In this method everyone who wants to can experiment with being the voice of the characters and symbols in the story and to interact with each other while staying in role. Earlier we spoke about the story of Sarah: God insisted that Abraham send away Sarah's servant, Hagar, who was Abraham's concubine, and Hagar's son. Toward the end of *parshat Vayera* (Genesis 18:1-22:24), an angel calls out to Hagar as she despairs in the wilderness, and she realizes there is a well within sight of where she and her son are sitting. A question came up in the bibliodrama: Who is the angelic messenger? Here is a *d'var Torah* that contains the answer they found:

> At first my Torah study group intensely disliked my Bat Mitzvah Torah portion, *Vayera*. Hagar has been put out of her home by Sarah, with God's approval; and after minimal resistance, Abraham consents. These are very disappointing ways for a matriarch and a patriarch to act.
>
> The Torah takes us out into the desert with Hagar. She is a person who has lost everything: her home, her job, and her beloved Abraham. She loses touch with a lot of important things about her life—for example, that she knows the region well and can surely find her way, that God told her when she was pregnant that her son would father a great nation, that Abraham showed caring by personally giving her food and drink and coming to see her off.
>
> Hagar becomes so severely depressed that she doesn't notice that a well is within view of their location. That is a sign of a very great depression. Sometimes people get so dangerously depressed that they can lose their hold on life. Hagar did. She set her son a bow-shot away from her, lifted up her voice, and cried out.
>
> One day, while imagining this scene, all of a sudden I became aware of a second woman coming into this scene. She is on a camel; her face is veiled; the camel is laden with water and food, and I sense piles of gold jewelry are also in its sacks.
>
> Suddenly, I know who it is on that camel. It is Sarah.
>
> Back in the camp, the just-weaned baby, Isaac, has been inconsolable at this loss of his big brother playmate and his nursemaid, who was also like a mother to him, Hagar. His wails awaken Sarah's heart. Sarah remembers that Hagar was her best friend, it feels like, forever. In her fears for her son and captivation with issues of power, she also has become dangerously out of touch with what is really important. She has sent her servant and longtime

companion to what could be her death. She has sent Isaac's beloved older brother off to die. What was she thinking?

So the angel, the messenger in the text who tells Hagar to look up so that she sees the well—my vision says this messenger was Sarah. Can you see that Sarah must have slipped out of the camp to go to Hagar to do *teshuvah*? Doing *teshuvah* means going to the person who has been hurt to discuss what happened, to accept responsibility for your role in it, and to try to reverse the damage in your relationship.

Sarah did what we all have to do when we hurt a friend: undo it. She also did a mitzvah that we have to do for anyone we know or love when they get very depressed: be with them. A severely depressed person can be a danger to herself.

What happens next? My vision says that Hagar comes back to her senses. She accepts the extra gifts from Sarah and recalls that she had long known her son would have to strike out on his own someday. And at thirteen, Ishmael was indeed the traditional age for doing so in those times.

Hagar now has the resources and the insight to go on. The two women beloved by Abraham now part company, each moving forward with a vision of her own son as precious and an important part of the future. After all, wouldn't they both have become Jewish, since they are in Abraham's life and mothers of his children? They are in Abraham's life and mothers of his children? It has been said that every Jewish mother wonders at least once whether her son could be the messiah.

Well, my tutor showed me a Hasidic commentary that takes the Hebrew word for messiah and breaks it into *mae-siach*, "from dialogue." So if my vision of Hagar and Sarah could be true, from a dialogue of sincere *teshuvah*, personal understanding, and inner change, they were able to resolve their situation in peace. May we all be blessed to be able to do this, to each be a little bit of a messiah ourselves, by engaging in *teshuvah* with our friends and neighbors day by day. Thank you.

This *d'var Torah* reveals an experience of *sod*, of mystery in the text being clarified; a portal to a new level of understanding has occurred. This deep *d'var Torah* also does three other things:

- Uses humor as a bridge to a powerful point
- Draws on a traditional commentary to incorporate ancestral wisdom
- Uses a sound bite of Hebrew to transform a concept that could seem very remote into something everyone can attempt

The Four Dimensions of Torah Study, the PaRDeS Model

Pardes means "paradise" in Hebrew. How do you think the ancient rabbinic sages would imagine paradise? A Jewish folk tale gives their vision of paradise as spending eternity sitting near the Tree of Knowledge in the garden of Eden learning Torah. Actually, we can all experience this kind of Eden in the here and now because paradise is a state of mind that can happen during Torah study.

In this chapter's examples, you have experienced the four dimensional model for Torah study called PaRDeS, which takes its name from the sound of the first letter of each dimension:

P'shat is the simple, basic story: who said and did what with whom, how and what came of it.

Remez are hints in the language of the text, such as metaphors that open up opportunities for deeper meaning.

D'rash are the missing dialogue and difficulties in the text that your imagination can fill in and so expand the inspiration and meaning.

Sod is the secret. What hidden meanings are embedded in the text that will help you relate to it today?

Take Careful Note of Names

Interpretive opportunity knocks within the names of people and places in the Torah. Names help tell the story.

For example, Exodus 19 mentions by name the places in the wilderness through which the Israelites wandered for thirty-seven years; these names appear nowhere else in the Torah. Each name has a root word that describes an experience; for example, the first is *Rimon Peretz*. *Rimon* means "pomegranate," and *peretz* means "burst." In modern Hebrew *rimon* means both pomegranate and hand grenade. This portion could contain the seed of opportunity for a *d'var Torah* on issues of territoriality in the Middle East.

Yitro (Jethro), the father-in-law of Moses, is a Midianite priest. This is an interesting opportunity to create a *d'var Torah* on intermarriage. Moses has married a Midianite woman. What will his relationship with his in-laws be like? The Torah gives us a clue, perhaps, because Yitro is also called *Reul,* meaning "friend of God." In fact, Yitro teaches Moses how to develop a leadership infrastructure so that he doesn't have to handle every Israelite who needs guidance or has a gripe himself. Many B-Mitzvah students have one parent who isn't Jewish, who is, at the same time, wonderfully supportive of the child or stepchild's B-Mitzvah process. This portion might create an entry point to speaking about this.

Learn About the Story's Culture and Time

Is there something about the culture of the time in which the story is set that you would like to know more about? Your *d'var Torah* might reveal surprising information about the biblical period. For example: Why does Sarah give her servant Hagar to Abraham so that he can get her pregnant? Isn't that polygamy? Or immoral?

Discovery: anthropologists have found tablets that reveal law codes of ancient Middle Eastern regional peoples permitting an infertile woman to stay married by providing a child to her husband through her handmaid.

There is a substantial world of biblical scholarship that ranges from revealing literary analysis by, for example, the works of Robert Alter to theological and anthropological perspectives, such as *Sinai and Zion* by Jon D. Levenson and *In the Wake of the Goddesses* by University of Chicago professor Dr. Tikva Frymer-Kensky, of blessed memory. Periodicals abound which can enliven Torah studies from the popular magazines *Moment, Hadassah, and Biblical Archeology,* to more scholarly options such as the *Jewish Bible Review.*

Turn to the Ancestors for Guidance

Our sages in their Torah commentaries are careful to point out interpretive opportunities in the text. Because the Torah was an oral tradition first, some stories even appear twice, with significant variations. The Torah also contains words on whose meaning translators can't agree and places where the sequencing is very strange. It is

Tip

Finding and Screening Mentors and Tutors

When considering tutors and mentors, seek those who have the ability to maintain healthy boundaries, physically, emotionally, intellectually, and spiritually. This requires a professional level of awareness. Don't assume someone has healthy boundaries, even if they have been in the educational system for a long time; there have been too many problems with clergy, teachers, and other professionals with boundaries of late. Keep a door open and have easy access to public space if you are an adult undertaking B-Mitzvah preparation. Parents need to ask pointed questions about what is taking place on days when they are not present. All students need to be careful not to flirt with, dress alluringly for, or otherwise tempt tutors and teachers.

Trope tutors aren't always going to be meaning-makers, those who delight in the study of Torah and making it relevant to living. You can have more than one mentor. Who gives a dynamite *d'var Torah* in your experience? Ask for their help in working on one. Who seems super into prayer at sendees? Interview this person; ask for guidance to help get into prayer yourself. Whose artwork on the Internet or locally inspires you to want to combine Judaism with art in your life? Meet with or correspond with this person. Involve this person in your d'var Torah or B-Mitzvah invitation or centerpieces. Seek all kinds of guides. People love to be asked!

Consider all kinds of venues for finding tutors and mentors: Synagogue staff, Jewish studies and Hebrew departments at area colleges, Hadassah, B'nai B'rith, and other organizations. Visit Jewish art exhibitions and museums, discover whose contemporary work moves you. Find that person and involve him or her in your life. Tutors can be of all ages—midlife folks and elders can volunteer to make Torah much more than a matter of rote memorization for our youth.

Jewish community centers increasingly have Jewish program staff on board. Spend private time with these talented professionals. They also do a lot of programming and will know who many of the multi-talented Jewish resource people are in your region.

The Wexner Foundation and Melton Programs are among those that fund and/or offer Torah study for Jewish communal professionals and active lay persons; you might ask one of their local program coordinators to help you find a mentor from among their students. Also contact Jewish Federation professionals. They might help you seek out tutors and mentors from among their increasingly learned leadership.

Ask regional and national Jewish retreat centers to post notes on their e-mail lists and bulletin boards for families who are seeking B-Mitzvah tutors. Often their teachers and students have great skills for this work.

Then screen, screen, screen. Check references; have initial meetings; and both trust your gut reaction and check in regularly with yourself if you are an adult learner and with young student(s) for progress and safety.

Tutors who work one on one with Jewish youth rarely receive training in how to do so. Bmitzvah.org & our sister site ReclaimingJudaism.org offer a two-year distance learning training in Jewish Spiritual Education, perfect for b'nei mitzvah educators to learn the methods and perspectives in this volume in greater depth while receiving individual supervisions. We also offer community programs for b'nei mitzvah families world-wide.

Make a mitzvah: visit Bmitzvah.org to fund a scholarship for your tutor to attend teacher and tutor trainings. Your family and future generations will benefit greatly.

traditional to start out learning the meaning of a given *parsha* in the company of the extensive notes of the commentator called Rashi.

Rashi, Rabbi Solomon bar Isaac of France (1040-1105), and Nechama Leibowitz of Israel (1905-1997) are perhaps the most widely read of the commentators who both address every Torah portion and are also available in translation. Rashi often explains difficult language and compares similar parts of the text in ways that open up all kinds of interpretive opportunities.

Nechama Leibowitz's legacy of commentary presents excerpts from Rashi on each *parsha*. She also harvests from the commentary of every significant sage who commented on the Torah before her death, comparing and contrasting their points so that you can see across the generations. Her commentary can usually be found in a seven volume set in Jewish libraries, along with many others. Contemporary commentary abounds in print as well as on the Internet, where it is most easily found by searching on the name of your portion, or a verse (e.g., Genesis 1:1).

Presentation Matters

How you give public presentations is going to matter all your life. This is your opportunity to learn effective presentation skills and debut them in front of an audience that loves you for who you are. They do not expect perfection; this is a debut, not a finale. You are there to help them take away something truly meaningful from their encounter with Torah. They are there to learn from you and witness how you've changed on the path of preparing for this moment. You are engaging in a rite of passage, becoming a teacher of your people.

Think of your favorite teachers. What makes their presentation style effective? Borrow from your role models. Let's look first at what you should do to prepare in advance for your presentation on your B-Mitzvah day.

- Stand like a teacher or speaker whom you admire. Does his or her style fit you? Practice in the mirror. What stance helps you make your points?
- Practice making eye contact when you speak in a small group. Notice how this means people turn toward you and pay better attention.

Tip

New Approaches for Learning to Chant Torah

Like many ancient civilizations, the Jewish people includes the chanting of sacred text as an important part of our ceremonies. B-Mitzvah students classically learn to chant their Torah and *Haftorah* portions and do so as part of their ritual.

At one time these ancient chants were preserved through a series of hand motions that correlated with specific musical phrases. The Masoretes, living in ninth-century Israel, invented a system of notation that allowed them to write down the music, a system we call trope. The Masoretes are the same scholarly school that invented vowel symbols, greatly easing our ability to read Hebrew

Chanting is designed to amplify the meaning of the text. A good example occurs during the dramatic episode in which Abraham is about to slay his son Isaac in Genesis 22:1–18. If you take a look at the trope for when the angel calls out to stay Abraham's hand, you'll find a trope pair called *kadmah v'azlah* that looks like two curved horns pointed toward each other hovering just atop the words. This pair of horns has the musical sound of a horn announcing the arrival of a king or the opening of a major ball game. That's the point of trope—to help tell the sacred stories.

The vast majority of B-Mitzvah students do chant some or all of the portion, depending upon ability. About half learn the actual notes, and half memorize by rote from tapes. Advances in technology now make it faster to learn the notes than to memorize by rote. Trope Trainer (Kinnor.com) is an exceptionally well-designed computer program for learning to chant Torah and *Haftorah*. This program lets you set the audio voice at male or female, change the key and pace, and simultaneously hear the music and see the trope, Hebrew, and transliteration. With such a program you can train yourself to know the musical notes for chanting sacred text with amazing ease and free up a lot of tutoring time to focus on finding meaning.

- Are there those whose manner of giving presentations in public you admire? Make mentoring dates to learn from them. Find out how they prepare themselves, their content, and their delivery. Ask if they will listen to you rehearse and help you fine-tune. People are usually honored and delighted to be asked to help in this way.
- Make handouts. Not enough *Chumashim* to go around at your service? Make photocopies of the text. Remember to use at least fourteen-point type; eyesight dims with age, and you'll have a very diverse community at your service.
- Have your own presentation ready, printed out in sixteen or eighteen-point type, double or triple-spaced, stapled together. You will know it so well by the time you get up there that you will look down only occasionally; the large type will make it easy to catch the phrase you need. The stapling will prevent last-minute spills from erasing the order of your speech. Knowing your material well in advance will allow your charisma to develop and shine through when you are in visual contact with your audience.
- Give at least one person who is definitely attending a backup copy of your talk and any other presentations you will be doing on your B-Mitzvah day. At the last minute, people often forget obvious things, especially those going through major life-cycle moments.

Dress matters. The Torah is wearing a crown, breastplate, and special cover. What will you wear to be taken seriously as a leader of prayer and teacher of Torah? You are meant to feel festively dressed to honor Shabbat, yet not be dressed in a way that takes people's minds off listening to your key points and lures them into thoughts about your physical appeal. What the B-Mitzvah initiate wears to lead services will often differ significantly from a party outfit for a major reception. You are setting the stage for a religious ritual; what you and others wear when ascending the bimah needs to be appropriate to this context.

Tip

Beyond Speaking

Don't feel that you have to limit your *d'var Torah* to the spoken word. Many renowned Jewish educators have employed the power of music in helping their audiences understand their unique perspective. Torah as a Tree of Life has inspired sacred song writers throughout the generations. The rhythm and beat of our times also reflect this motif.

Rabbi Margot Stein's recording "Create Out of Nothing" includes a magnificent rendition on saxophone of the *Eitz Chayyim* Hee, "She Is a Tree of Life" prayer traditionally chanted while putting the Torah back into the ark. (Mirajtrio.com)

Rabbi Shawn Israel Zevit's *Yah Eloheichem Emet* track on his Heart and Soul CD helps bring the message of mitzvah of caring for the stranger profoundly into the heart of prayer. (http://www.cdbaby.com/Artist/ShawnZevit)

You can texture your *d'var Torah* and service with the burgeoning world of new Jewish sacred music. Because most people derive a great deal of comfort from the melodies that have become traditional in their synagogue, take care not to overwhelm your service with new music. You will likely find a warm welcome for two or three new melodies. And if you create a special service booklet to hand out to your guests, you can make participation more comfortable by placing the lyrics inside with a note telling them how to acquire music by the composer. Also see: URJbooksandmusic.com

Following are some points to help you on your B-Mitzvah day.

• Find a smile deep inside yourself and let it shine through at appropriate times when you are about to speak, during your presentation, and afterward. A sincerely felt smile speaks volumes into the hearts of those present in under a split second.

- Speak slower than you believe is necessary. Those listening haven't seen the text; it takes them time to absorb your points from sentence to sentence. Breathe between phrases; look around at those present; take your time.
- Use body language. Move your hands and your head; step out from behind the lectern. You are not in a photograph. Live, from your town; it's your B-Mitzvah!
- When you stand up to give your talk, pause at the microphone. Breathe three times slowly; relax your shoulders; adjust your papers, your glasses, and the microphone. Feel comfortable in your stance. Look around at those gathered; find eyes of those you treasure and smile. Now begin.
- When you finish your *d'var Torah*, pause. Look around at those present. Breathe. Then with dignity enter the next step of your ritual.

This chapter has answered in many ways the question of why the *d'var Torah* is a significant milestone in the transition to an adult role within your Jewish community. This is your special time to shape the future by passing the light of Torah through your highest self. Share your vision, views, values, and voice with the *minyan* of your life. Your people want to hear your voice, to know you are learning our sacred texts and traditions, and that you are able to bring an important and new *d'var Torah* based on your studies and your perspective. Now you have many tools and ideas. Go for it; you can do this and shine!

Chapter Six

Exploring Mitzvah Project Options

*B*ar/Bat Mitzvah (B-Mitzvah) students, by definition, are engaged in learning and practicing mitzvot, the basis for living a meaningful Jewish life. An expected part of this process is for the student to identify and take on a special mitzvah project that contributes to advancing justice in the world. A mitzvah, commonly known as a commandment, is a sacred act done with consciousness. Among the mitzvot are many categories of behavior essential to the maintenance of civilization and to the advancement of health and happiness for all. Although Judaism heavily encourages learning Torah and tradition, it is for a purpose: to inspire you to action.

Mitzvot often involve deeds, like supporting a blood or bone marrow drive to save a life, raising funds for social welfare or cultural life in Israel, and caring for the environment. Other mitzvot are accomplished by self-restraint, like not acting on the impulse to steal, lie, or murder. A person who is ready to become B-Mitzvah knows how to live as a Jew and actively seeks out opportunities to fulfill mitzvot.

At the heart of our faith is the principle that changes for the better are possible. Judaism does not say that you have to be perfect, nor are you personally responsible to make it all better, nor will those things made better necessarily stay that way for all time. Creation continues; earthquakes take place, and we help the survivors to recover. A new disease, like AIDS, emerges, and we help to fund research for prevention, treatment, and cure. We are all partners in the process of creation.

It is a principle of "our tribe" that we strive to do our best to contribute to the quality of life for all life forms that we encounter. The dolphin, the neighbor, the river, the stranger, family, teachers, and friends—for these life forms and more, we care and act, hoping to give and receive justice and loving-kindness.

There are many levels at which mitzvot take place. Each is a way for you to improve things between:

(continues on page 159)

The Missing Mitzvah Feathers

A bag of colored feathers was missing from the retreat supply shelf. We were with Project Kesher in Ukraine, invited by a local group of Jewish mothers and their daughters to teach them what Judaism is. These mothers and their mothers had grown up under communism, when any form of the practice or study of Judaism was punishable by imprisonment.

The bag of colored feathers had a simple purpose, to be something light in my luggage, unusual to the local culture, and memorable to signify the preciousness of our time together. Who had appropriated the feathers at the last minute? It wasn't necessarily a theft. We had told everyone that all the supplies were available throughout the retreat for projects related to our teachings.

Not one retreat participant had ever experienced a Jewish wedding, lit a *menorah*, or had the option of a *Bat Mitzvah*. It had been a week of tears of loss and tears of joyful recovery and discovery of the beauty of living a Jewish life. I had just finished our last teaching unit, on the importance of noticing and acting whenever a mitzvah opportunity arises in your daily life. Students had shared many examples of how they could help others spontaneously throughout any given day, and I had sent them out of the room with encouragement to seek out mitzvah-making opportunities in every room they enter.

Next, I went off to ask the staff about the feathers and found my answer while passing through the dining room. Children from the region of the Chernobyl nuclear plant meltdown were the other occupants of the sanatorium we were using as our retreat center for the week. Desperately ill with leukemia, many of them were covered with sores. We had been requested not to interact with them, to leave them to their own fresh air retreat funded by their government. The staff had taken down mirrors at the facility, citing a belief that it was acutely depressing for the children of Chernobyl to look at themselves.

In the dining room, I found our girls, the feathers, and the children of Chernobyl.

Our young retreatniks were prancing through the dining room decorating the children with the colored feathers. Under communism femininity was symbolized by a strong and homely caricature, similar to that found on Arm and Hammer Baking Soda boxes. We had arrived just as cosmetics were being rediscovered by Soviet society. I watched our girls opening their treasured powder compact cases and the children of Chernobyl beginning to behold themselves in the mirrors. As the sanatorium staff rushed over to implore me to get our girls under control, to close those mirrors, I shushed and implored them to look and reflect within themselves before acting on old orders.

You see, for the first time that week, the solemn, sick, sad children of Chernobyl were smiling, hooting, laughing, preening, and even prancing in delight. Eventually, one of our girls saw me looking on and called to the others. They came running up to us, beaming as she found enough English words to express her inner light to me: "Reb Goldishkeh, Reb Goldishkeh! We Jewish girls, we have just made our first mitzvah!"

CREATING A MITZVAH-CENTERED LIFE

Place a check mark in each box that is an appropriate answer for your relationship to each mitzvah listed below.

Mitzvah	Meaning	A Good Mitzvah to Try or Continue This Year	Want to Learn More About This	Not Just Now, Another Year
Bal Tash-hit	Living with environmental consciousness			
Shalom Bayit	Adopting ways that yield greater peace at home			
Shmirat Ha-Guf	Treating your body as sacred space; good food and care			
V'hadarta P'nei Zaken	Honoring the experience and needs of senior citizens			
Shmirat Lashon	Speaking ethically, guarding against gossip and slander			
Pidyon Sh'vuim	Redeeming captives			
Tza'ar Baalei Chayyim	Preventing cruelty to living things			
Ma-ah-chil R'evim	Feeding the hungry			
Yizkor	Remembering those who have died whom you knew			
Ezrat Cholim	Helping those who are ill			

CREATING A MITZVAH-CENTERED LIFE

Place a check mark in each box that is an appropriate answer for your relationship to each mitzvah listed below.

Mitzvah	Meaning	A Good Mitzvah to Try or Continue This Year	Want to Learn More About This	Not Just Now, Another Year
Neechum Aveylim	Providing appropriate support for those in mourning			
Kashrut	Being conscious of eating, food production, and preparation			
Heshbon Ha-Nefesh	Reflecting on one's deeds and errors, seeking insight			
Kibbud Av v'Em	Giving honor to living parents			
G'nivat Da'at	Promoting truth in advertising			
Mezuzah	Marking your home and work place as sacred space			
Ahavat Tzion	Working for the well-being of Israel and her citizens			
Leyshev Ba-Sukkah	Taking your meals in a sukkah			
Pikuach Nefesh	Doing what it takes to save someone's life			
Hachnassat Orchim	Treating all those around you as your guests			

CREATING A MITZVAH-CENTERED LIFE

Place a check mark in each box that is an appropriate answer for your relationship to each mitzvah listed below.

Mitzvah	Meaning	A Good Mitzvah to Try or Continue This Year	Want to Learn More About This	Not Just Now, Another Year
Shabbat	Connecting with loved ones, community, and God one day each week without work and with sweet rituals			
Minyan	Showing up to create Jewish community			
Tefillah	Keeping a rhythm of expressing the prayer of your heart			
Limud Torah	Using Torah as a prism for growth and awareness			
Teshuvah	Working honestly with hurts to heal a relationship			
Hadlakat Neirot	Welcoming Shabbat with candlelight and blessings			
Al Tifrosh Min Ha-Tzee'bohr	Not separating yourself from the community			

These spiritual practices are available as a beautifully illustrated deck titled "Mitzvah Cards" through Amazon.com

- *You and yourself:* one example would be by caring for your body with better food, rest, and exercise, and showing respect for your body and spirit as you explore your sexuality and gender.
- *You and the inner circle of your life:* for example, by engaging in the mitzvah of *teshuvah*, where you and someone who has hurt you or whom you have hurt try to work out a better understanding so that your relationship and hurt places can begin to heal.
- *You and strangers:* by working on some facet of making sure that there is food, clothing, housing, education, honorable work, safety, culture, and community available for all.
- *You and nature:* by simply not polluting, by learning how to better care for the environment, by teaching others, and drawing attention to species needing help to survive.
- *You and God:* through prayer, festivals, Shabbat, lifecycle events like baby namings, B-Mitzvah, Jewish weddings, and other religious acts that help you feel awe and gratitude at creation, to develop an appreciation of the precious, limited gift of time and life.

This chapter will help you discover the joyful, life-giving power of mitzvot. Here you will find many solid examples of personal and social action-oriented mitzvot that have proven successful and can serve as guidance on how to focus and refine your own mitzvah efforts during this precious period of preparing to become B-Mitzvah.

Focusing Your Mitzvah Goals

Three distinct categories of mitzvot apply directly to being ready to become B-Mitzvah.

- Personal. Judaism intends for you to texture time with practices that soothe and shape the soul, recognize history, and create meaning for living. Personal mitzvot affect your relationship with God and make time for your understanding of God to expand and serve your spirit. This category includes experiences such as attending services; feeling more blessed by saying blessings at meals, upon seeing a rainbow, and other appropriate times; growing through Torah study; having an *aliyah*;

putting on *tefillin*; saying *Kiddush* and observing Shabbat and festivals; putting up a mezuzah; lighting a *menorah*, and engaging in other such activities.

- *Gemilut hassadim*, "deeds of loving-kindness." These are powerful personal actions that improve the quality of life for all beings: visiting sick and lonely persons, cleaning up the environment, working on healing relationships, lobbying to enact laws to secure health care benefits for all, helping someone find a mate, creating animal sanctuaries and homeless shelters, doing volunteer work at home through projects such as Habitat for Humanity (Habitat.org), taking on assignments available through your local Jewish Family Service or congregation or overseas through the Jewish World Service (JWS.org).

- *Tzedakah*. Giving money is called *tzedakah*, "justice," because the equitable, fair, and honorable redistribution of funds is the only way that everyone in the world can survive and thrive. No amount of volunteer work cancels out the Jewish obligation to give money generously within your ability to do so. People often suggest that everyone should really be able to take care of themselves. Many, it turns out, literally can't.

Millions of AIDS orphans roam the street of Third World nations with no one to raise them; famine, flood, earthquake, civil war, and fire wipe out homes and workplaces worldwide. Prejudice, patriarchy, and caste systems leave millions of women and children without rights, homes, government policies, health care, literacy, or prospects for survival in lands like India, Afghanistan, and Egypt, as well as much of Africa and Southeast Asia.

At present, even in developed nations like Israel and the United States, over thirty-four million citizens live below the poverty line. Many elderly people who responsibly saved all their lives for their old age are running out of rent and food money because interest rates have dropped so low that they have to use up every penny to survive. In some states electric companies still can turn out the lights and not deliver heating fuel when a household runs out of funds.

Even if all a Jewish person can afford is a dollar, we give; it is our way. A Jew doesn't leave people alone to struggle in the dark, whether that dark is literally being without money for food or fuel, without

Tip

Leverage Your Mitzvah

You can become a more savvy donor to causes by seeking out a community fund that will give you a *tzedakah* bank account and match your giving with substantial funds, often hundreds of dollars, from a foundation, business, or community fund.

Consider participating in or creating a youth philanthropy program in your community. These projects help youth to do the following:

- Understand the magnitude of need in the world
- Experience the crucial value of their own giving to leverage essential services, training, care, research, and hope for others
- Learn how to serve as responsible philanthropic committee members, to collaborate, listen, reason, give, and vote

Although businesses have been matching funds for employee philanthropy for some time, now youth philanthropy programs are springing up everywhere. These are fun, exciting, and educational.

Many youth philanthropy funds offer trips to see worthy causes in action, emphasizing how they work and what it takes to keep them going. Often youth get to pool their funds with other participating peers and then serve as an allocations committee that studies causes and votes on how much to give to which groups. Some of these groups also hold donor parties or races and hands-on projects to support and celebrate what youth can accomplish by giving together.

The Jewish Federations of North America website, UJC.org, offers links to many excellent youth philanthropy programs. One such, the Jewish Fund for Justice, JFJustice.org, also offers an excellent curriculum about the roots of poverty for use in religious schools.

literacy, or without safety. We also greatly value culture and learning, the advancement of civilization through support for schools, colleges, and cultural institutions.

There are four major ways to give *tzedakah* during the B-Mitzvah process.

• An important step in the journey of B-Mitzvah is for the student to give some *tzedakah* money from the student's own pocket, by means that you devise and not from funds given or allocated to you.

• Many also take a significant percentage of the cash gifts they receive at B-Mitzvah and donate this to good causes. You know it's enough when the amount feels like a genuine sacrifice for you and your family.

• It is also customary for friends and family to honor someone becoming B-Mitzvah by making a donation in the student's honor. People appreciate help and encouragement to undertake *tzedakah*. You have the power of the pulpit and can point out causes that attract your concern and suggest them in your invitation, *d'var Torah*, or thank-you speech. Let your guests know that you will consider support for causes a most valuable B-Mitzvah gift, that you and your family will feel greatly honored if support for change in the world is given in your name.

• In honor of your B-Mitzvah, it is customary for you and your family to give something to your worship community that improves the temple, religious school, or religious life in some significant way that fits your economic reality. This might be donating to a school or Israel-trip scholarship fund; purchasing a new pointer, a *yad*, for reading from the Torah; buying a new Torah cover, a Torah, or prayer books; donating a jungle gym to the nursery school; giving shelves, books, or CDs to the library; purchasing a long-needed coat rack for a temple hallway; or funding a grant to bring in a scholar or artist-in-residence. Ask the staff; they'll know best what's needed. All worship communities are nonprofits, and dues barely scratch the surface of what they need.

Fulfilling Thirteen Mitzvot

There are several major models for engagement in mitzvot for B-Mitzvah students. All recognize that moving into empowerment as a Jew involves learning more about some of the very difficult parts of life—poverty, disease, war, child labor and forced prostitution, illiteracy, refugees, abuse, pollution—by meeting and participating in helping people and programs that address these painful problems.

Israel's kibbutz movement originated this model, wherein a student is helped to identify thirteen mitzvot to undertake throughout the year of B-Mitzvah preparation. These can be an assortment of mitzvot that relate to you, your relationship with God (for example, through Shabbat or prayer), your family, your community, the Jewish people in particular, the environment, and the planet. In this model one need not launch a major independent social action project; rather, the goal is to expand experience in a wide variety of mitzvot.

Batya, who lives in southern Florida, decided this model suits her personality and abilities best. Here are the thirteen mitzvot she selected to work on during her *Bat Mitzvah* year:

1.   I will encourage my family to take me to visit my Aunt Sara in New Orleans more often this year. She has become a widow and is not adjusted to being on her own. (Mitzvah of caring for the widow)

2.   My older sister is very sensitive about her acne, and I made fun of her in front of her boyfriend. I will let her know I have realized this was mean and intend not to do so again. (Mitzvah of *teshuvah*, relationship repair)

3.   I heard the neighbors complaining that the halfway house for people with severe learning disabilities needs painting and is running down the neighborhood. My sister is in the synagogue's teen youth group, and I am going to suggest to her that they could hold a painting party and help fix the place up. (One who helps make a mitzvah is credited with the doing of it.)

4.   Each year on some nights of Hanukkah, we forget to light the *menorah*. I will take charge of not forgetting. (Mitzvah of lighting the *menorah* and telling the story and meaning of the light)

5.   There is a used winter coat drive in our town every year. I will call ten classmates at home and ask their parents if they would be willing to donate any extra winter coats. Then I will ask my cousins who have drivers' licenses for a ride to pick up the coats

and deliver them to the collection center. (Mitzvah of caring for the poor)

6.   I will ask for a mezuzah to put up on the entrance to my bedroom and also for the back door, which doesn't have one yet. I learned a mezuzah is meant to be on every doorway of a home except for the bathrooms. (Mitzvah of mezuzah, treating your home as a sacred place)

7.   Every week I am going to save one dollar from my allowance and begin the regular practice of buying Jewish National Fund trees for Israel. These funds go for trees and efforts to help restore the fertility of the land. Roots hold the topsoil so that the wilderness can be reclaimed and the fertile crescent restored. (Mitzvah of *ahavat tzion*, loving care for the land of Israel)

8.   I have never been on a *shiva* call, a visit to the family of someone who has died. I will accompany my mom or dad the next time they go so that I can learn how to do this with dignity and overcome my fears. (Mitzvah of *neechum aveylim*, comforting mourners)

9.   I will ask my dad to take my grandmom and me to visit my grandfather's grave. I want to tell Zeyde [an affectionate Yiddish term for grandfather] about my *Bat Mitzvah* and imagine he is giving me a blessing. (Mitzvah of *yizkor*, remembering the dead with honor)

10.   The Jewish Federation has a mitzvah day every year. I will participate in one of the many mitzvah opportunities they offer. (Mitzvah of *al tifrosh min ha-tzee-bohr*, being careful not to cut oneself off from the community)

11.   My mom has been wondering whether to have gifts for her fortieth birthday party. I'm going to suggest that she ask everyone who can to write an $18 check in her honor to the scholarship fund at our school. (Mitzvah of *tzedakah*, of donations to support)

12.   I learned from Danny Siegel (DannySiegel.com) that dry cleaners have unclaimed clothes. Next time my dad stops with me in the car to pick up his dry-cleaned shirts, I'm going to ask if they'll give us their unclaimed clothes to take to the homeless shelter on a regular basis, since they posted a notice requesting donations of clothing. (Mitzvah of *gemillut hassadim* , deeds of lovingkindness)

13.   I will wake up in the morning and say the morning prayer for getting up, *modah [f] modeh [m] ani l'fanecha melech chai v'kayam,*

which asks us to wake up full of praises for the gift of life. And I will think of one thing or quality that is a great part of my life every day and whisper, sing, or dance out my thanks for it! (Mitzvah of *tefillah*, a rhythm of meaningful prayer)

One Major Mitzvah Project

Exceptional B-Mitzvah students have undertaken many magnificent and substantial projects. And perhaps equally many have intended to do major projects and found the year of B-Mitzvah preparation to be so full that things got started too late to fulfill what were really good intentions. This model requires the following:

- Sufficient maturity to see a task to completion over time
- An early start
- Creation and fulfillment of a detailed plan
- A support team of perhaps three persons who understand the student and who appreciate the goal
- For youth, a supervising adult mentor, specifically someone capable of guiding without taking over the actual planning and doing of the mitzvah

Caution: It is actually demoralizing and a source of shame for a young person to announce a major project and discover he can't fulfill it due to lack of time, experience, transportation, and so on. And it is unfulfilling for the student, if a parent ends up doing the project to get it over with and out of the way or to get the requirement checked off on a religious school's must-do list.

Following are some examples of major mitzvah projects.

Advocacy for Justice

In order to be effective and yet not miss too much school, Dylan and his mom went on three days of a week-long cross-country Freedom Ride bus trip sponsored by an advocacy group concerned about the terrible working conditions that immigrant workers suffer.

Dylan took photographs to document what they witnessed and wrote a newspaper article about what he saw.

Dylan and his mom brought copies of the photos and articles to the local paper and met with their senator and congressman to ask for support for legislation on the issue.

The school newspaper carried Dylan's story and photos; the local paper carried his photos and interviewed Dylan about his experience.

Deeds of Loving-Kindness

Wendy's best friend's mom had cancer and four children under age ten. Her dad was working two shifts to make ends meet, and housekeeping really wasn't happening. The synagogue's *Hessed* (Loving-Kindness) Committee set up a system of congregational volunteers to help transport the mom for treatments, prepare meals for the family, and keep house.

Wendy organized a laundry squad of three B-Mitzvah girls from her class. Twice a week until the mom recovered, Wendy and her team went over to do the laundry. They worked out an agreement to walk or bike over. With a key they let themselves in quietly through the back door and left the laundry folded on top of the dryer when it was done. The girls did homework and sang together, becoming what they call "best friends for life" while they waited through the cycles.

Tzedakah Project

Sandra read on a website that for a loan of around three hundred dollars, a poor woman could start a small business of her own in places like Ukraine and Bangladesh. This concept, called micro-loans, might involve making it possible for such a woman to be able to buy a sewing machine, computer, or espresso machine so that she could make a living instead of selling herself into prostitution due to her mounting debts. Sandra resolved to raise enough funds to contribute to a nonprofit loan fund in order to support one woman.

Sandra researched several nonprofit organizations that encourage such micro-industry projects and found a Jewish program, Project Kesher (ProjectKesher.org). She called their U.S. office, learned about their loan program for women to start their own businesses, and saw that she could realize her goal through them. Sandra even received a report of the many fascinating projects for which Project Kesher had given loans in the past year.

Sandra decided she would crochet *kippot* and sell them for ten dollars each through the synagogue gift shop, with a negotiated percentage of the sale going to the synagogue, until she had raised the three hundred dollars with her own labor. She succeeded in her goal in six months, and by the time of her *Bat Mitzvah* had raised enough to support two women. The added beauty to this model is that the women proudly repay these no-interest loans, and thus each success multiplies the number of loans available.

Class Mitzvah Projects

Some communities have mitzvah projects that have become traditions that one B-Mitzvah class hands down to the next. Your class might take on a project similar to these.

- Planting and tending an herb garden for the blind or a healing garden sign-posted with inspiring messages, set perhaps in a county park. Each year's B-Mitzvah class does the garden's fall and spring cleanup, replaces plants as needed, takes shifts to weed and water the garden, and repair or replace signs made in Braille and conventional print for visitors. In some cases a class raises funds and dedicates benches and sculpture and helps with expanded landscaping, for perhaps a contemplative walk for those healing from a major illness or facing great stress.
- Serving meals at a homeless shelter or creating regular events, perhaps storytellings or sing-alongs for the children's wing of a hospital or senior adult center.
- Collecting unused technology for others to use. One inspired class collected working, unused recording devices from local families and donated them to an inner-city school where impoverished immigrants struggle to learn English after work. The recorders allowed the effectiveness of the immigrants' home studies to soar.

Tip

Establishing Mitzvah Mentors

Despite all the need out there, figuring out how to make a mitzvah that will be personally meaningful and right for this stage of a given student's life is not always obvious. Here are some suggestions.

Call up and interview someone whose mitzvah work you really admire. Find out what she does, how she got into it, and how she can help you find a mitzvah that fits with your talents and skills.

Are you part of a class or youth group? Invite area nonprofits to send over someone active with them who will serve as a member of a panel of mitzvah mentors for your group each year. Invite this person to speak to the youth and adult B-Mitzvah classes at a congregation, day school, or summer camp. Ideally, each student would find and work with an agency whose mission corresponds best with the student's talents, interests, and ability.

Organizational bulletins and newspapers can carry mitzvah opportunity listings just as they do want ads. Invite each nonprofit in your area to post mitzvah-maker want ads on the bulletin boards of your community spaces, websites and classrooms. Ask them to list a mitzvah mentor for each task whom interested students can call for guidance.

Create a mitzvah registry. This could be maintained by the area board of rabbis, the Jewish family life educator on staff at a local Jewish community center or Jewish Family Service, or by the synagogue-relations task force at your local Jewish Federation. Youth require a lot of supervision for mitzvah projects to succeed. At Philadelphia's Jewish Family and Children's Service, Rabbi Nancy Fuchs-Kreimer, author of the book *Parenting as a Spiritual Journey*, helped created a program called the Youth Mitzvah Corps in which B-Mitzvah youth volunteer and receive training, supervision, and recognition for doing various kinds of important work within the region's Jewish and non-Jewish agencies. The Jewish Coalition for Service coordinates mitzvah service opportunities around the world for all major Jewish organizations and all ages (JewishService.org).

In addition to checking with local congregations and social welfare agencies, adult and college B-Mitzvah candidates might check with their local Israel consulate or community *shaliach* ("representative" from Israel, who is usually found at a Jewish community center, day school, summer camp, or Jewish community relations council) for help with identifying project opportunities in Israel. Links to local *shaliach* offices are available on JAFI.org and also consider the New Israel Fund (NIF.org)

- Collecting, repairing, and selling used bicycles. Often bicycles that have become too small accumulate in classmates' garages; select the best of these for sale at a consignment shop after your class works on cleaning them up. Arrange with the shop to donate a hefty percentage of each sale to the charity of your choice; perhaps the shop owners will even put a percentage of their own earnings from the sale toward the charities you select.
- Providing essentials to people in shelters. Battered women who leave home for safety often flee without even a toothbrush, nightshirt, or underwear. Some B-Mitzvah classes restock such centers with these items, even hand-painting messages of self-care and support onto the nightshirts for mothers and their children.

Rebecca, an adult B-Mitzvah student, undertook an unforgettable and substantial project. The daughter of her next-door neighbor was the victim of a suicide bombing. The mom was a single parent, the mother of three children; her husband had died two years before on military reserve duty. The children were adopted by their aunt and uncle. When Rebecca's neighbor put her house on the market in order to raise money to help the aunt and uncle care for the girls, Rebecca learned that the girls' extended family was really unable to take financial responsibility for dressing them or provide them with any educational or play things.

Rebecca called a meeting of the parents and students from her class in public school and from the B-Mitzvah youth and adult classes in her religious school to ask them to help out. Most families signed up to be part of a rotation to obtain and send seasonal school and play clothes, and also to buy books and toys for the girls. Rebecca faithfully maintained the rotation chart, stayed in communication with the family, and arranged shipping. She found another B-Mitzvah student to chair this project after her. Rebecca became a mitzvah mentor to the chairperson, as well as making visits to inform, support, and encourage the new B-Mitzvah class in successfully continuing this project.

By now your plate is quite full with learning and projects sufficient to create a B-Mitzvah preparation year filled with growth and blessing. It is time to contemplate what it will be like to celebrate the many accomplishments you are beginning to set in motion. The next chapter offers many unique ways to share the joy of attaining B-Mitzvah with your community, family, and friends.

Chapter Seven

Joyful Jewishing: Approaches to Celebrating

I t is a mitzvah to provide a celebratory meal and entertainment for your guests. This party also honors the B-Mitzvah student's hard work and accomplishments in preparation for a meaningful life of mitzvah-centered living. Our sages ruled long ago in the compendium of Jewish law called the Shulchan Aruch that B-Mitzvah is every bit as much a *simcha*, "joyful occasion," as a wedding and declared that having a *seudah shel mitzvah*, "meal of the mitzvah," is indeed an authentic component of the mitzvah of B-Mitzvah.

Yet another mitzvah is embedded in the party and process of having family and friends come to witness and celebrate with you from distances near and far. This mitzvah draws on our Middle Eastern origins all the way back to Abraham and Sarah and is known as *hachnassat orchim*, "welcoming guests," a process that is gracious, comforting, and filled with attention to detail. From invitations to accommodations to appreciations, the challenges of offering hospitality on a fairly large scale await most of those preparing a B-Mitzvah.

It is often said that the B-Mitzvah party is a rite of passage for those who prepare it. Moving from making a mitzvah by attending to making a mitzvah by hosting is in itself a major life-cycle transition. Given that one is piling the stress of planning the party and receiving guests atop the many activities of daily living, its realistic to experience these matters as rather daunting. This chapter will help ease your way with systematic guidance and support for finding and sustaining your vision for creating a memorable party.

How Festive Is Appropriate?

This is a question that families and communities often ask. Let's reframe this question: What kinds of festive are appropriate? A glimpse back in time to before World War II can help with this line of inquiry.

In Eastern Europe's thriving Jewish culture, *klezmorim*, or village musicians, would bring the passion and pathos of Yiddish music, lyrics, and dance to every *simcha*. There was the Broom Dance, the Mitzvah Dance, many "klutz" dances—and at weddings, even a dance for having married off your last child.

And let's not forget the *badhanim*, the "rhymesters, clowning and satirizing, diversely skilled, sometimes bardlike characters who moved through Jewish parties lightening hearts with newly worked gems and favorites for which the audience would call out. Some were also fine magicians, making doves appear and watches, scarves, and kopecks disappear.

Other *badhanim* had keen political and relationship satire as their comedic bent. In every age the Jewish political and social condition is somehow still distinct from those of other peoples. It is helpfully healthy to be able to mock ourselves lovingly; on Purim it is even a religious obligation.

Skillful humorists who can be clever without being cruel can contribute to making a great B-Mitzvah party. Of a desirable *badhan*, it has been said that no guest should leave the presence of such a one with "dry eyes or dry pants." Clearly, full-bellied laughter is indeed meant to be part of a Jewish party scene!

In some times and towns, graphic artists are known to have been present among the after-Shabbat B-Mitzvah party entertainers. (Some Orthodox communities consider the human image to be *b'tzelem Elohim*, in the "image of God," and so they do not allow capturing that image through art.) Among popular items were silhouettes of guests that the artist made on the spot, cutting them out from black paper and presenting them to each enchanted recipient. Caricaturists captured truths in a few insightful and swift hand-waves of charcoal. Another take-home memento might have been the image of a whimsical cat or the like captured in tatted lace or needlepricked tin; or an elaborate paper-cut image of a Torah, Lion of Judah, Star of David, or other such symbols.

To this day a Sephardic tradition is to decorate with henna, a temporary red dye, the celebrant's arms, hands, and sometimes feet and cheeks with regional symbols for good fortune, birds, and flowers.

Then there were the storytellers: *maggidim* (Hebrew) or *dertzeylerin* (Yiddish). Imagine how the children would fly over when a storyteller entered a party, just far enough into festivities to be perfectly timed for reddening eyes and sore little feet. Can you hear them begging for favorite stories, settling down on the floor in a circle with eyes widening in wonder at the newest tale?

And guests offered many toasts in honor of and descriptive of the B-Mitzvah initiate's qualities, the challenges the student had overcome, and appreciation of familial hospitality. Some toasts were invited in advance; many more were given when a guest rose spontaneously from his or her seat, hoisted a glass on high, and offered praise that rang truthful and straight from the heart.

In some regions guests were expected to bring their own compositions of poetry, music, or skits to entertain the B-Mitzvah initiate, who was placed in a seat of honor.

Neither was there a shortage of complementary popular culture from outside Jewish life; classical pieces and regional folk dances were generally welcome. The magic was in the mix.

And who ever forgets being lifted aloft in a chair, quaking with joy and release at being honored by those who really matter most!

Although the B-Mitzvah student likely opened the meal by chanting the *Kiddush* prayer over the wine and Hamotzi prayer over the bread, the closing blessings for this magical day would likely be the *Birkat HaMazon*, the blessing of the nourishment, given perhaps by an uncle with an

Tip

Creating a Vibrant Simcha

To the extent that you are able, you might help create an enduring mitzvah out of your B-Mitzvah by founding at your local synagogue, Jewish community center, or Jewish Federation a *simcha*-centered cultural panel and fund. This would become a registry for *klezmorim*, Sephardic and Israeli bands and vocalists, as well as instructors of Israeli, Yiddish, and Eastern European folk dance, Jewish humorists, storytellers, creative artists, and others. Such a fund could make it possible for families to hire high-quality Jewish entertainment for culturally oriented simchas, with repayments to the fund set up on a sliding scale.

Some report it was indeed a tradition before World War II for an affluent family to send an entertainer, artist, one or more *klezmorim* or humorists as a gift to the parties of those less well off in town. What an amazing act of *hessed*, "loving-kindness," such a gift is, one that brings dignity and joy while nourishing the cultural repertoire of our people.

If you contribute to this kind of initiative and are involved with a local synagogue or Jewish youth movement, make sure that a Jewish folk dance troupe is helping students in the religious school, day school, and youth groups to discover some of the high-energy dances within our tradition. Too many times those at a B-Mitzvah know how to dance only a *hora*; an expanded repertoire really will liven things up.

operatic voice or the community's cantor, *hazzan*, who would belt it out in power and beauty.

Perhaps some of the traditional elements just mentioned speak to your developing vision for entertainment at the *seudah shel mitzvah*, the meal celebrating the one who has become B-Mitzvah. And yes, there is plenty of room to include elements of popular culture. Throughout Jewish history our people's life-cycle events have often included components representing the larger cultural settings in which we live. Ragtime, swing, jazz, rock--new cultural evolutions of music--were and are welcome and often expected complements to creating an atmosphere of celebration at a Jewish life-cycle event.

The real trick is getting a satisfying balance of general and Jewish culture so that a B-Mitzvah party retains a memorably Jewish character and clarity of purpose that distinguishes it from a secular party event.

Reviewing Goals

During party planning it's essential to remain in touch with the goals that have become dear to you in this process. Everyone at your B-Mitzvah is relearning from your choices what a Jewish celebration can be like; generations may replicate what you do. It's very worth doing this with consciousness.

Your goals and objectives will need to be writ large in your consciousness because coming your way is an entire service industry with its own bottom-line needs and vigorous assumptions that reflect and sometimes create regional social trends. To achieve the quality of family connection, celebration of Jewish culture, and memory-making moments that yield inner happiness and satisfaction after the B-Mitzvah party can require moxie on your part. Even simple amendments to usual party practices can meet with surprising resistance because successful businesses are appropriately designed to repeat their own norms and standards of service.

So how can your party be truly special and deeply reflective of your goals and objectives? Start by making sure that you prepare logistics to support all the dimensions of your plan and design preparations to fit within your budget. Here's an example of one family's discussion with a caterer of a goal many people have in mind:

Family: We have such a large set of family and friends and yet want to create a climate of effective social intimacy, which will encourage those present to get to know each other and increase our ties to one another.

At the last few parties we attended, it was really only possible to meet those sitting on either immediate side of a person because it was impossible or absurd to shout across the huge central expanse of the circular table. Our hosts had set us there, near interesting people, with great forethought; and yet those across the table were simply out of vocal reach. And because of the table's centerpiece, we couldn't even make visual contact. It was actually quite boring sitting there and difficult to keep coming up with conversation to the same two people.

For the B-Mitzvah meal, let's have rectangular tables with seating for eight people instead of circular tables that seat ten. It's always easier to meet and talk around the narrower rectangular tables. And also let's agree on a buffet; people will talk while they're in line. We'll be sure to encourage people to switch seats during the meal.

Caterer: Elegance demands large circular tables. That's what people expect; that's what we stock; and surely it's what you want if you really think about it. And waitpersons are part of elegance as well; besides you don't want family elders and the children spilling platters as they cross the dance floor. We provide exceptionally professional waitstaff.

Family: Maybe we could settle for a schmoozing place away from loud music where the family could interact. (Away from smokers, lest only they can use it.) We'd need some cocktail-size tables, a waitress, and drinks over there. But the schmoozing-place model doesn't really fit our intention fully. Can tables that will meet our original goal be rented elsewhere? And we definitely want a buffet; that helps people to get away from their tables to socialize. Please make some calls and get back to us.

Caterer: I made some calls; since we don't own that size and shape, it will cost eighteen dollars extra per table to do this.

Family: We'll get back to you once we have the full cost-benefit picture and we are in a position to make detailed decisions.

This family will have many more planning decisions to make. It is usually better to delay and batch up decisions that will have an impact on vision and budget for an upcoming family team meeting. While interviewing caterers, this family found several could offer better rates because they already carry the desired table size and shape, so they were able to resolve the matter easily. Notice how having a well-crafted mission statement and goals makes a satisfying process possible and gives the family the strength of spirit to get what they require.

It can be strikingly helpful to give your B-Mitzvah Action Plan (BMAP) mission statement (see Chapter Two) to the vendors you are considering and ask them to frame their proposals in light of it. Some families share their full BMAP with chosen vendors. You will quickly know if you want to work with a given company based upon the quality of their responses.

Covering Your Bases

OK, you can see there are many possibilities for claiming your power and creating a very exciting B-Mitzvah party. Let's get to some basics before soaring into many more specifics. The primary components of party planning will include what usually turn out to be several segments of a weekend. The planning team will need to think through each of the following points thoroughly:

1. Location of your B-Mitzvah service and reception
2. Invitation list and tracking of replies (including guests' time of arrival and transportation to lodging)

3. Lodging for guests (especially for those who do not travel on Shabbat)
4. Meals, including special meal requirements
5. Appreciation and souvenir gifts
6. Task chart outlining who does what and when

Location of Service and Reception

You can hold your B-Mitzvah service and reception any number of places: the synagogue, your home, a retreat center, an arboretum, even in Israel. Wherever you choose, book space at least a year in advance; in most communities event space is tight.

On what day will the service be held?

- Monday or Thursday (Torah is also read on those days)
- Friday night
- Shabbat morning
- Shabbat late afternoon
- Prior to and including *Havdalah*, the closing ceremony for Shabbat that involves brief melodic blessings, a beautiful braided candle, a cup of wine, and fragrant spices as symbols

While Shabbat morning is usually most appropriate and satisfying, sometimes the other options are needed due to a unique local or personal situation.

Invitation and Replies

What theme and what medium do you want for the invitations? Should they be printed? E-mail invitations are becoming popular, as they are better for the environment. Which guests might benefit from receiving a personal telephone invitation so that they'll feel comfortable coming?

You'll need to set up a tracking list for responses. Who's coming to which parts of the B-Mitzvah weekend? What are their special needs? You'll also want to track the gifts they've given so that you can send detailed thank-you notes.

Keep track of guests' planned times of arrivals and provide options for transportation to lodging. Which guests do not travel on Shabbat?

They will need lodging close to the service and reception if that will be on Shabbat.

Directions to services, meals, and meal times need to be printed and either included in the invitation or sent by e-mail or regular mail to those who will be attending.

Lodging

The B-Mitzvah host can book blocks of rooms for out-of-town guests at discount rates. This needs to be done about half a year to a year in advance. If your event will be held on Shabbat, keep in mind that some guests do not travel on Shabbat and will need lodging within walking distance of the service and reception.

Meals

Which meals will you organize or provide?

- Friday night dinner
- *Oneg* Shabbat dessert or light meal for congregants and guests after services
- Shabbat breakfast
- Shabbat luncheon or lunch reception
- Shabbat *seudah shelishit* (early evening meal before Shabbat ends)
- Saturday night reception
- Sunday breakfast or brunch

Are there special meal requirements for any of your guests? Keep in mind that Sabbath observers cannot use transportation or money on Shabbat and so will need kosher food available throughout the day.

Appreciation and Party Favors

Remember to provide small presents or lovely notes for those who volunteer special support such as hosting guests in their homes, making food, picking people up at the airport, mentoring, tutoring, and so on. Some families also provide party favors for every guest.

Task Chart for an Easier (& Greener) Celebration

Set up a task chart outlining the tasks to be done and specifying who is responsible for each. What needs to happen and with what supplies? How will it be set up? When? Who will be doing it (vendors, professionals, or volunteers)?

Here are additional tasks and details you may want to see to (Try to use recyclable materials wherever possible):

• Judaica: You will need a *kiddush* cup, *challot* (the plural for *challah*), *kiddush* wine, and song and perhaps blessing booklets. Some will want hand-washing stands with ritual washing cup and towels, a *Havdalah* candle, and spices.

• Do you have a rabbi or cantor working with you? Will you need someone to help lead services and blessings for all or some of the B-Mitzvah events?

• What about entertainment? Weaving Israeli, modern and ballroom music, dance and dance instruction, comedy, and art-making are all possible choices.

• If you're using a printer, you'll want to plan the invitations, thank-you notes, place cards, and prayer and song booklets.

• You'll need to plan for food, beverages, cook(s), perhaps a caterer and waiters and waitresses.

• Arrange transportation from and to train, air, and bus terminals.

• Prepare decorations and comfort measures, such as setting out guest towels, flowers, and tissue boxes in the bathrooms. (Potted flowers which family and guests can take home afterwards are better for the environment.)

• Arrange for supplies for the B-Mitzvah meal: tables and chairs, tablecloths, china, glasses, silverware, serving utensils and bowls, chafing dishes, and so on. Buy these on-line and after the party donate them to a non-profit and take a tax deduction for the donation. Win-Win!

• Will you hire a photographer or a videographer? When, where, and who? Will you provide disposable cameras on every table for guests to take candid shots?

• Will you (or the venue) provide an area for child care and caretakers for restless or overtired little ones?

Tip

Keeping Track

Effective on-line invitation and guest tracking tools are now available. These products have become very reasonable and save time. Starting out this organized will make your process much easier.

Components to check for include the following:

- Ease of tracking individual guest contact and title details
- Ability to print labels in a nice calligraphic font
- Ability to record invitation responses
- Notation space and reports for gifts received and thank-you notes sent
- Sections for listing guest accommodations and travel arrangements
- Place to note service readings, aliyot, or other helpful or ritual roles guests will take
- Ability to create seating charts and easily print seating and name cards
- Option for tracking vendor contact information
- Option for tracking vendor bids, bills paid, bills due, and the event budget
- Ability to create simple reports and summaries

- Try to be more present. Secure serving and clean-up assistance.

Involving Friends And Family

The "*minyan* of your life", i.e, your inner circle, will be happy to help; trust and empower them. By inviting trustworthy friends and community members to help out, you can actually have the space to experience the sacred, precious quality of this time and allow them to make a mitzvah by helping you.

Families are borrowing a major Jewish tradition about this from the Jewish wedding, where the bride and groom select a *shomer* (male) and *shomeret* (female), usually a dear friend or close sibling, to help during the twenty-four hours leading up to the wedding. For the B-Mitzvah, you too can ask a friend to shadow appropriate family members as a personal assistant, answer the door and screen phone calls, vet interruptions from often overzealous photographers, run for the extra safety pin, listen with understanding to last-minute jitters, and so on.

Whether your event will be held at home or in a major institution, assigning friends and community members to the following positions is also helpful:

Greeters and ushers at services and meals

Transport liaison, someone aware of who is arriving and leaving and can help guests have a smooth experience

Party captain(s) to communicate with a professional party planner, if you have chosen one, to meet the vendors as they arrive, watch for quality control, and make sure refills take place

Someone to monitor the photographer(s) to ensure the unobtrusive experience for which you are hoping

Parking attendants who can help ease the way, doing *hachnassat orchim*, welcoming guests

Gift table attendants, who make sure gifts dropped off are labeled with a tag to identify the giver

Coat check station to cut down on chaos and help folks feel welcome

Chaperons to maintain boundaries for young adults at your event

Caution: Sometimes unsupervised young adults tend to form a group and head out to unused rooms or behind the building for experimentation with drugs and physical activities that the host never intended to sanction. This is a widely reported phenomenon. You are the responsible party and need to be prepared. The nature of the entertainment does not seem to limit this from happening. Transport, such as a van or a bus to collect young guests, will need just as much monitoring. Set boundaries for your event and maintain them.

Involving The Community And The B-Mitzvah Class

Starting in the twentieth century, a well-intended new B-Mitzvah policy began to cause occasional problems. Congregations required families to invite all the classmates of a B-Mitzvah student to the family party, not just their closest friends. Although this was intended to prevent hurt feelings among classmates, families sometimes found that having a fairly large class present at the party proved to be in tension with the goal of encouraging family to get to know each other better. Most families are widely dispersed due to the mobility of our times; the advent of a *simcha* is a serious opportunity for family bonding. In addition, taking responsibility for a large number of youth and still feeling present to your own event is difficult, as is taking on the expense of the obligation. Good solutions to this dilemma are beginning to emerge. One is for parents of a given B-Mitzvah class to organize a monthly, quarterly, or annual class party to celebrate everyone who has had a B-Mitzvah during that interval.

Another is to have the congregation agree that B-Mitzvah parties will customarily be a potluck event after the service. Each family can thus invite everyone in the community and have help with preparation and entertainment. The economic stresses of major B-Mitzvah parties have led some to drop out of the B-Mitzvah process rather than risk feeling humiliation at not being able to compete with affluent families. This model puts everyone on a more equal, dignified, and mutually honorable footing. With good planning the amount of fun to be had will not require copious spending.

In some places families hold two separate and very different parties, one for the class and congregation and another for closest friends and family.

Roots And Retreats

Taking the family away from the local scene and on a retreat for the B-Mitzvah has both serious merits and challenges. A retreat is a very major planning project that maximizes your opportunity to create your own approach to B-Mitzvah and offer many opportunities for family and friendship ties to develop. Many summer camps and retreat centers will take offseason bookings for just such family *simchas*. This is a fairly easy way to manage the catering side of matters because room and board are usually part of the plans such centers offer. Given the presence of sports facilities and the often-stunning locales, groups usually have ample room for informal and spontaneous activities, easily accessible Shabbat naps, and even family-led Torah study and song in addition to your B-Mitzvah service ritual. On the other hand, planning a retreat is a labor intensive undertaking. The staff at Bmitzvah.org often consult on creative B-Mitzvah options; this site is provided by a non-profit and there is no charge for this service.

Israel offers roots-based adventures for B-Mitzvah families. Keep in mind that the Western Wall may not be open to mixed-gender prayer, gatherings, or religious rituals for girls and women. However, beyond the many magnificent natural and archeological settings, *kibbutzim*, and museums are excellent choices usually hospitable to a wide range of denominations. In some years the Torah reading cycle in Israel is a week off from that in the United States, so an Israel B-Mitzvah decision needs to be made early or the student could find belatedly that he or she has prepared the wrong portion! Judith Isaacson and Deborah Rosenbloom have written a rather complete book dedicated to this subject—*Bar and Bat Mitzvah in Israel: The Ultimate Family Sourcebook*.

Caution: Should you opt for an out-of-town B-Mitzvah, keep your home community in mind for some simple ritual that will honor them and let them honor the new status of the B-Mitzvah student when you get back. You can accomplish this by scheduling an *aliyah* to the Torah during services and sponsoring an *oneg* Shabbat (light reception after services), a scholarly lecture, or a cultural event. Another option is to have the B-Mitzvah initiate offer a slide show and talk about the trip and ritual experience for your home community.

Upping The Energy

One caution first: monitor the volume. Teens are losing their hearing from severe decibel levels at parties and adults can't take it and become dispirited because it's impossible to socialize. Moderation prevents hearing damage and allows guests of all ages to better build community and enjoy themselves.

Upping the energy often involves supplementing the power of the microphone from party DJs and bandleaders and setting in that place the *tummler* of your choice. *Tummler* is Yiddish for hell raiser" or "inciter," and more often affectionately means someone who understands the culture of your family and guests and who, as mistress or master of ceremonies, can lovingly get them up and involved in a fullness of celebration.

Do you have a *tummler*-type in your family, among your friends or community? Engage this person to help out at the microphone.

A South African B-Mitzvah tradition worth adopting is the way best friends of the initiate put on a play about their friend in the middle of the party. These skits can be memorably sweet and funny, and they are a wonderful way to keep the focus of the event on what and who is being celebrated.

Take back the microphone from the professionals even more by inviting family members in advance either to tell three-minute stories from family history or to recall moments in the initiate's life that bring the fullness of who she or he has been and is becoming to light. This works best when all the talks are not batched together; rather, arrange to have maybe three or four at a time, then more eating and dancing, followed by another batch. In a three-hour party, one set per hour works well.

Your *tummler* or dance instructor might organize a circle dance that invites different groupings of guests into the center of the circle; this helps people know who is present early on. "All the cousins into the circle. . . . Now all the friends from school. ... Now all our friends from the Sierra Club. ... Now everyone who has ever been to the land of Israel. . . . everyone who is from the mother's side of the family. . . . now from the father's side" and so on. Celebrate your guests; let them feel how much it means to you that they took the time out to attend.

Tip

Photography

When selecting a photographer, screen for manner as much as outcome. Some photographers move out in front of the participants as though thinking themselves invisible, and this blocks the guests' view of what is happening and so damages the energy of the ritual.

If you do hire a photographer, insist that he or she move about unobtrusively and take lots of candid photos with a low light capable digital camera, so that you can post easily to the web and send the website address to those who couldn't make it.

Insist that the photographer use no flash. This really disturbs the ritual.

Because of some photographers' pricing policies, it is essential to negotiate in advance that you will receive the images on a CD or via the web, own them, and have the right to print and send them yourself.

Emphasize that candid shots will be the most interesting and memorable. In fact, screen for photographers who are capable of taking candid shots, which require a different eye than shots that are set up.

Schedule a dress-up portrait-taking session, if you desire, a week or more before the B-Mitzvah. Think about it: How much sense does it make for a young person about to lead his or her first service to spend the hour before services having pictures taken? And taking pictures directly after the service can take the glow right out of a person. These are precious moments that you all have been preparing for, for a very long time. Treat them tenderly.

Avoid photography between the service and the party; this can push everything off schedule. The first time a photographer seems out of line to you, very firmly tell him or her to fit in as asked; become as pushy about this as needed. It usually pays to assign a friend to monitor the photographer to ensure the unobtrusive experience for which you are hoping.

While most will use cellphones, it's also fun to place disposable cameras on the table for guests to take their own shots. Collect these cameras before guests start leaving. Some may inadvertently take a camera home with them, so also put a label on the camera with instructions for where they can send the camera to you.

Also having a videographer? Try this:

Announce that question cards are on each table that are designed to trigger memories about the B-Mitzvah initiate and the family. Ask guests to find one question from those on the card that she or he can answer on video by sharing a brief vignette.

Assign teen anchorpersons time slots to circulate with the camera person. Hold a training session with your young helpers before B-Mitzvah day, and then turn them loose at a designated time at the party to hold what can become quite memorable interviews.

A note on video, photography, and the B-Mitzvah service: One of the principles of Shabbat is that nothing new gets made on the day of rest. So to capture a Shabbat service on camera is really to miss out on one of its big, beautiful points. What happens on Shabbat is ephemeral; it is feelings and memories—within. Guests won't necessarily know this about Shabbat; a note on your service booklet about your preferred rules regarding photography will prevent embarrassment on their part and annoyance on yours. Flashes going off during a service are especially inappropriate.

Seriously consider providing name tags that reveal where a given person fits into the scene: friend from religious school, grandfather of the B-Mitzvah, just in from New Zealand, and so on. Families are so spread out these days that we need help with forming connections.

Consider The Advantage Of Themes

When we talk about themes, we're not talking about the fabled (we hope) family who had each table and food station designated as a different department store chain, as though a B-Mitzvah were some kind of celebration of the North American retail business. There's a powerful world of stimulating themes right inside of your planning, self-assessment, and d'var Torah preparation processes. Your selection of themes necessarily precedes the ordering of invitations, selection of music, design for centerpieces, and the like. Here are some examples.

Talent

Seth is passionately involved in tennis, playing it and watching it. At first he wanted a tennis theme but realized that was more appropriate for a birthday party of his youth than a celebration of his Jewishness. His tutor introduced him to the Maccabiah Games, world-class Olympic-style games for Jewish athletes from all over the world, which take place every four years in Israel. Seth found the concept fascinating and wove the theme throughout his B-Mitzvah.

Invitations were crafted from a photo of a Maccabiah awards ceremony, with Seth's face placed among those in the crowd chanting "Torah! Torah! Torah!"

Each centerpiece at the reception was a cake that served as a base to hold an enlarged photo of a Maccabiah award winner and an inspirational quote from the person.

Seth's Torah portion was about the wilderness wanderings of the Israelites after leaving Egypt. Seth reflected on how the slaves developed an identity during their period of retraining for freedom and how they learned to function as a team in the process of becoming a more self-disciplined and principled people. He then spoke about how sports had helped form his character, how much the discipline of sports helped him to know how to focus on preparing for B-Mitzvah, and how he saw the Jewish people as needing to view themselves as a team. Seth spoke about his grandfather, a Holocaust survivor, who would often come out for Seth's games.

He then spoke of how important it was for him to learn about the Maccabiah Games, to discover there are many sports-minded Jews who take seriously the need to be strong, healthy, and a source of pride for our people. Seth declared his intention to attend the next Maccabiah Games and began to learn about how he could prepare and enter a season of Maccabiah Games himself.

Seth's family had quietly informed those on the guest list of a plan to create a group gift, a fully paid trip for Seth to view the next Maccabiah Games in Israel. Everyone supported the idea so strongly that he was also able to help sponsor a player.

Metaphor

Melanie's B-Mitzvah theme came from the prayer that begins, *or chadash al tzion ta-ir,* "A new light will shine over Zion." Melanie conceived of each B-Mitzvah student as a new light and also became interested in the rebirth of Jewish life in the former Soviet Union as new light. Here's how this theme appeared throughout her B-Mitzvah.

Her invitations showed Melanie as an *Or Chadash,* a new light, by having a *menorah* upon them with all the candles lit except for one on which her smiling face was set in the shape of the flame.

For centerpieces the family placed a mirror in the center of each table and a beautiful, metallic candlelit *menorah* upon it.

Melanie's mother is active in Project Kesher, an organization that has helped Jewish women throughout the former Soviet Union who are interested in reclaiming Judaism. The program also helps women avert poverty through computer skills; it works on issues such as stopping the trafficking of women for prostitution and spreading awareness of domestic violence. After the B-Mitzvah, Melanie's family sent each *menorah,* something too costly for women in the groups to acquire themselves, as a gift to a Project Kesher community.

Melanie started her party as Ben and Sara did, with *Havdalah,* the closing ceremony for Shabbat that includes the strong light of a multi-wicked, braided candle. (For more details about the meaning of *Havdalah's* symbols and creative approaches to the ritual, see *Reclaiming Judaism as a Spiritual Practice, Volume One: Holy Days and Shabbat* by Rabbi Goldie Milgram.)

At the party Melanie's father took the microphone to speak about her special light, and soon many family members came up to express similar sentiments illustrated by memorable vignettes, as well as recollections of family members long gone also blessed with a special light of their own.

Melanie's invitation included a card asking for donations to several organizations, and she sent notes of appreciation with a candle flame on each one and a line of appreciation thanking her guests for making possible an increasing light in the lives of so many people.

Sacred Phrase

Adam's Torah portion, *Terumah*, has the phrase *nedivat lev*, "generosity of heart," in Exodus 25:2. The context is that the vessels for the tabernacle must come from the people's voluntary donations. Adam took this to mean that the sanctuary within each person is created by one's generosity of heart. Adam worked with this theme in several ways.

He called everyone to the Torah who had signed their organ donor cards; at the same time, he invited everyone to come up for the *aliyah* who had not yet signed their cards and wanted to find the courage to do so. He blessed them for their courage to give others life.

At the reception all of the coffee cups were mugs from the regional organ donation center, bearing cutely meaningful slogans and graphics.

His invitation and party had heart motifs and included a donation card for the regional organ donation center, with a request that guests donate in lieu of bringing gifts.

Adam's family had difficulty with a synagogue policy requiring that all religious school classmates be invited to B-Mitzvah parties. This policy had worked well when the temple was smaller to ensure that some students wouldn't feel left out. But this year's B-Mitzvah cohort of fifty-three students would overwhelm the family-centered vision for his B-Mitzvah party. The family dealt elegantly with the situation: in honor of Adam's B-Mitzvah, they hosted a class trip to the regional organ donation center, paid the honorarium for a local Jewish expert to teach the class about the mitzvah of organ donation (Judaism greatly encourages saving a life so long as the gift does not compromise the donor's health), and took the class out for felafel afterward.

For his mitzvah project, Adam volunteered to run an e-mail campaign to help find a bone marrow donor for a local youth—and he succeeded!

Adam used thank-you cards from the organ donation center, in which he wrote personalized messages.

Symbol

Kaela had the story of Noah as her portion and selected the rainbow as her theme. She loved her rabbi's interpretation of the rainbow that appears in Genesis, that it is composed of God's light passing through God's tears.

Israel

Matt, a budding scientist, came from a family many of whom were displaced persons after World War II, who made it to live in Israel, and had many losses in its wars for survival. Matt's *parsha* was *Shelach Lecha*, Numbers 31:1-15:41, where Moses sends twelve men out to investigate the promised land and bring back reports. Two return bearing grapes and good reports, the rest bring fearsome data. Matt decided to take up the importance of being able to discover good things in the land. Matt's party was filled with every good Israel-made food and object, poster, and invention that anyone could possibly obtain to reveal in a party setting the ingenuity of the people of Israel.

Genealogy

The begats were all over David's Torah portion. He decided the message embedded there for him was to learn to help his family reclaim their own genealogy as a theme throughout the B-Mitzvah process. JewishGen.org is an excellent research site for this work, as is Arthur Kurzweil's book *From Generation to Generation: How to Trace Your Jewish Genealogy and Family History*.

Sacrificial System

The trick with such portions is to look at what aspect of human life a given sacrifice is meant to attend. Some sacrifices and offers are to help us in dealing with critical issues of guilt, error, and broken promises regarding the mitzvot. Many parts of this system emphasize gratitude for the harvest.

Cheryl seized on the image of the waving of the wheat as a portion of it, called an *omer*, is delivered to the priesthood to support them with food. Cheryl came up with a cornucopia to reflect this part of her *parsha*.

Mazon (Mazon.org) is one of many Jewish initiatives to help those who are hungry, and Cheryl organized for her family to give 3 percent of the food cost at the party to help feed others.

When Imperfection Strikes

After so much thought and hard work, suppose something goes wrong at the B-Mitzvah party? The expectation that everything has to go exactly right places a great deal of stress on everyone involved in a *simcha*. Our people have a philosophical expression, *yad Elohim ba-kol*, "the Hand of God is in everything," which leads to a unique way to handle the unexpected. Let's observe how one family put this in action.

It finally happened to a family. Their son's *parsha* was *Ki-Tissa*. This *parsha* includes God writing out a replacement set of tablets and Bezalel being appointed head artist for the tabernacle that will house them. So it was only natural to take *yad Elohim*, the hand of God, as the B-Mitzvah theme.

The *hamsa*, the Middle Eastern symbol for the hand of fate, appeared on the invitations and the cover of the service booklet. The family donated a beautiful pointer for the Torah reading to their temple in honor of their son's B-Mitzvah, and of course Isaac used it to read his portion. The *d'var Torah* spoke about ways to notice with awe how the hand of God can be found outstretched through others, when, like Moses did with God and the Israelites after the golden calf incident, we go back to someone with whom we have stress and shift our behavior so that we call out their higher qualities.

Most exciting in the planning process was the time the family spent working with an artist to plan nine unique ceramic *hamsa* centerpieces for each table. Each would be a real work of art, and the hosts would give them out as a gift of appreciation at the end of the party to family and friends who'd helped out the most. This was a very special touch indeed.

Only the *hamsa* centerpieces never arrived. They just didn't.

For the mother who'd been most involved in this project, not having the centerpieces was like having a splinter under a fingernail.

The whole body might be well, but one little thing like that takes all your attention and keeps you from thinking of anything else. The rabbi saw distress on the mother's face and stopped beside her to learn of the problem. He understood.

"What an exasperating disappointment for you," he noted with empathy.

"It really is," she responded. "A lot of planning and pride had gone into this."

The rabbi replied: "Do you know the story of the dropped car keys? You see, a family was out on their boat on a beautiful day when the mother leaned over to point at an amazingly large fish when—splop—her car keys fell out of her top pocket and sank rapidly into the bay.

"Mother, what shall we do? How will we start the car to go home? How will we get into the house? We will be late for karate lessons this afternoon! Mother! What do we do now?'

"The mother looked at her sweet, concerned children, then up at the sky, down at the now-calm waters, and said: 'When you drop your keys in the water, I know what to do! Go right ahead and enjoy a beautiful day.'

"And somehow, with those words, this not only became totally possible, but it became a philosophy her children would live by for all their lives."

As the rabbi finished his story, Isaac's ever-outgoing Aunt Lara moved to the front of the room and quieted the band.

"Rise, and turn your eyes to the entry," she said. "Welcome a Jewish young man across the threshold of your life, a young man who has labored seriously and today become *Bar Mitzvah*!"

The mother's eyes swam with tears as she saw her son appear in the doorway. She let go of worries, refocusing instead on the preciousness of each moment.

When asked later what they thought of the centerpieces, any number of guests replied: "I'm sure they were wonderful. Everything the family did that day was beautiful and special." They hadn't even noticed!

Hiddur mitzvah is a Jewish principle that it's a mitzvah to adorn or decorate a mitzvah. So creating a beautiful B-Mitzvah party with delicious food, great entertainment, and fascinating decorations is actually a principled act when one does it with the levels of consciousness you have just studied. This is an exciting time to become B-Mitzvah; so many creative options are open to you. Party hearty—you've earned it!

In our final chapter we'll present some ways to enhance the process of giving and receiving gifts, organizing some touching rituals for yourself and other family members to engage in before the B-Mitzvah day, and then we'll close with some guidance on retaining and reviewing your upcoming harvest of B-Mitzvah memories.

Chapter Eight

Contemplating Heartfelt Blessings, Gifts & Memories

Daniel went home and unwrapped his *Bar Mitzvah* presents. His mom found him sitting dolefully amidst the crumpled wrapping paper and open envelopes. He was surrounded by many high-quality watches, several personal music and game players, assorted games, twelve gift certificates, and thirty-six checks.

She wondered at his mood and asked: "What's wrong, son?"

Daniel's answer: "I don't know mom, but somehow this is disappointing. This stuff just doesn't mean anything to me." Daniel is absolutely right. There are many ways to give *Bar/Bat Mitzvah* (B-Mitzvah) gifts that can touch a person's spirit, not just by way of a charitable organization. There is nothing wrong and everything right with receiving a physical gift so long as it adds meaning to the experience and expands the relationship between the recipient and the giver in a healthy way.

This chapter offers both traditional and unusual approaches to gift giving. And finally, lest the last thing that happens in the B-Mitzvah process is the writing of thank-you notes, we'll look at ways to harvest and protect your precious B-Mitzvah memories.

Creating Legacy Gifts

Many items in life can become legacy gifts. Even if giving a check has to happen because it's customary or sorely needed, also consider creating a special moment to give something personal and uniquely memorable. Start by looking into the contents of your life.

Are there pictures of great-grandparents or other ancestors that you can frame with a dedication plaque giving their names and dates in honor of the B-Mitzvah? Do you have stories about them to share in a one-to-one meeting with the B-Mitzvah student? Also write down the stories in your gift note or mount them on the back of the picture.

Consider the picture together with the B-Mitzvah student. Gifts become more meaningful to the recipient by the manner in which we convey them. Together notice details of dress, similarities perhaps between the student and the ancestor(s); if you can, explain about the period in which the photo was taken.

Is there something around your home that has always fascinated the student? Something he or she asked about or played with during visits? That could be the perfect gift.

Is there something that symbolizes a turning point in your own life that carries an important story and that you can give over as a sacred

The Silver Ring

Two weeks before Gail's *Bat Mitzvah*, Libby, her mother, said, "I have something special for you. Can you meet me in my bedroom in front of the jewelry drawer in a few minutes?"

Once there, Libby lifted out a small velvet case and passed it to her daughter. Inside lay a silver ring with a turquoise stone in it that had cracks filled with drizzled gold. "Gail Mara Milgram, this is my *Bat Mitzvah* present for you. This ring is full of special memories and it comes with a powerful blessing."

Libby slipped the ring onto her daughter's right-hand ring finger. It was a perfect fit.

Gail was thrilled, and she also had questions. "Mom, what kind of memories? And what do you mean, it comes with a blessing?"

"As you know, dear, during World War II, I worked as secretary to the surgeon general of the United States. Prior to moving to Washington, D.C., to help with the war effort, the only places I'd visited in life were in New York, where I grew up. So for my first vacation as a young working girl, I decided to do something daring for those times, to travel with a girlfriend to see the Southwest and observe how the native peoples live.

"It was a glorious and fascinating trip. I witnessed their tribal and religious rites, tasted new foods, and saw landscapes I could never have imagined. While there, I fell in love with this ring, bought it, and wore it every day until years later when I got married and replaced it with my wedding ring. "So I am passing this ring to you, in honor of your upcoming *Bat Mitzvah*. I am so very proud of you, of how hard you have worked, how much you have learned, and how beautifully you have prepared your chanting and *d'var Torah*. And I hope you will always be very proud of our people, the Jewish people, and treasure our practices and customs. I also hope we've taught you to marvel at the beauty of this world and the cultures of the many peoples who dwell within it.

"Gail, in giving you this ring, I bless you to have many wonderful travel experiences. And I hope that wherever you go, you will represent our people with honor and seek out Jewish connections."

The ring became part of Gail's life, and the blessing proved very effective. It is the only present I, the author of this B-Mitzvah book, once named Gail, now known as Goldie, can remember from my own *Bat Mitzvah*, though surely there were others. It still connects me to my mother, to the blessing (indeed, I've been privileged to travel the world), and to my *Bat Mitzvah*. And it still fits.

trust? This might become the cornerstone of a mentoring moment that will long resound within the student's memory. You might also find a novel or nonfiction work that relates to your point. You can then inscribe it, and give it to the B-Mitzvah student as a personal resource to hold on to until it is fully needed.

Jason's paternal grandfather died before Jason could remember him. His Aunt Wendy brought him one of his grandfather's leather books of poems by Walt Whitman, complete with notes Jason's grandfather had handwritten in the margins when he was young. The inside cover contained a dedication showing that Jason's grandfather had himself received the book as a B-Mitzvah present from his father. To Jason, this book is the greatest treasure he's ever received.

Allison's grandmother noticed a beaded drawstring bag in the back of her closet. She had the bag repaired and added the words Allison's *Tallit* Bag in beadwork. She presented Allison with the *tallit* bag at the party, with stories about some of the events that bag had been through with her.

Jenny's cousin obtained *Hadassah and Life* magazines from the day Jenny was born, thirteen years before that, and thirteen years before that. As the cousins pored over the magazines together, they were amazed at the kinds of advertising, events, and social changes they read about. Alice's mom helped her encase these magazines in sturdy plastic covers to preserve this unique gift for future generations.

Adam's neighbor discovered that Adam loves science fiction. On-line at JewishLights.com he found a series of Jewish science fiction books and gave Adam three as his gift, with the suggestion that they both read and discuss the works. One story discussed whether a nonhuman alien could convert to Judaism. This problem captured Adam's curiosity and led them into a whole new level of exploration.

Kerri's tutor had a big surprise for her. She picked up a plain beige suede *kippah* at the Judaica store and with fabric paint made a scene of Jerusalem on one half and an image of an open Torah scroll on the other half. Then, with a permanent marker, she wrote a verse from Kerri's Torah portion on the open scroll and Kerri's name in the very center of the *kippah*. On the inside she wrote, "Love to my fantastic student forever—your tutor, Dona."

Many Ethiopian Jews participated in an embroidery project to raise money for food, health care, education, before their immigration to Israel. Their high-quality, brilliantly colored *tallitot* and *tallit* and pillow covers interpret many Torah portions; their *mezuzot* also make stunning legacy presents and support their education and training in Israel.

Ari's classmates and their parents got together to acquire the series of Ethiopian pillow covers as a present for him. This proved to be so special that many classmates are hoping the same gift will be coming their way, too. It is also possible to twin with an Ethiopian Jewish immigrant to Israel, to share B-Mitzvah dates, correspond, and one day even to meet. The legacy of friendship is a very powerful gift indeed.

For information contact the North American Conference on Ethiopian Jewry at NACOEJ.org.

Special Activities As Gifts

Consider some activities that you can do together to privately honor this special time.

Ben's uncle took him to the steam room at the Jewish community center and proudly introduced him to the men who gather there after the men's weekly bagels-and-lox brunch. They joyfully welcomed him and shared stories of their own B'nei Mitzvah.

Sara's mom took her to a Judaica shop to select a set of candlesticks of her own to light every Friday night. She also told Sara a secret, that whenever she lights candles, she senses the presence of her own mother, of blessed memory. Also, when she blesses Sara, she senses her own mother's hands upon her head in blessing.

Kate, his mother's best friend, brought Max to a ceramics studio so that they could make a *challah* plate together in honor of his B-Mitzvah. On the back of the plate, Kate wrote a special signed message from her heart that was sealed there for every Shabbat to come.

Blaine's grandmother is an excellent needleworker. When she learned about a German Jewish needlework tradition called a whimple, she and Blaine agreed that making one together would be very

Tip

Creating Heirlooms

Precious things that can be passed along have to start somewhere. Family or friends might consider making a gift that can become a family heirloom, perhaps by taking an art class during the season of B-Mitzvah preparation. You might make gifts such as these:

- Judaic quilt
- Torah binder
- Siddur cover
- *Kippah*
- Mezuzah case
- *Tallit*
- *Tallit* case
- Jewish holiday table runners
- *Challah* and matzah covers
- *Sukkot* welcoming banner
- *Afikoman* bag

Other ideas might include appliqueing a box to hold a dozen Shabbat candles or a carved wooden *gragger*, "noisemaker," for Purim.

Jewish legacy art projects can be done quietly as surprises or together with the student as a bonding memory. Either way, the extra effort you go to will likely never be forgotten.

memorable. The whimple involves creating a Torah belt, to be used only on the special occasions of a person's life cycle that take place at the Torah. Traditionally, these would be started in honor of a birth, and the fabric would be derived from the baby's swaddling cloth. The belt is made up of multiple panels and is perhaps six inches wide. As each major life-cycle event arrives, each panel of the belt gets decorated in fabric paint or embroidery with the birthdate, name of the child, symbols, and a verse from that week's Torah portion or blessing. Antique and contemporary examples are on view at many Jewish museums.

Another collaborative craft project is creating a Judaic blessing quilt. One person sends squares of fabric to friends with instructions to return the decorated square in honor of the person's *simcha*. Nadine, the yoga partner of Talia's mom, decided her gift would be to coordinate such a project. Not being a quilter herself, she took the squares she had received from participants to a professional for assembly. Squares can be decorated with just about anything: fabric markers, buttons, necklace charms, shells (be sure to use fabric glue that tolerates washing). Messages from Torah, qualities about the student's life, or blessings can be added, too. Some even sew in tiny music chips so that a melody will emerge when the curious push on the squares.

Robert's father collects Israeli stamps. Over the years they would marvel together over the engravings and discuss the ideas that each of the stamps represented. In honor of his son's B-Mitzvah, this father asked if Robert would accompany him to a stamp convention and if he would like to begin collecting seriously in his own right.

The opportunities for meaningful engagement in gift giving are endless. What unique approaches have you experienced? Post them to Bmitzvah.org for all to see.

The Power Of Blessings

Your own blessing is one of the most important gifts you can bestow. There is an enduring tradition for Jewish parents to call their children to stand before them at Shabbat dinner or services and bless them with a traditional formulation:

For girls: "May you be like Sarah, Rebecca, Rachel, and Leah."
For boys: "May you be like Ephraim and Menashe."

Why Ephraim and Menashe and not Abraham, Isaac, and Jacob—or all of the sons of Jacob who became the tribes of Israel? There are three

Miriam's Cup

Kari's cantor, *Hazzan* Amy, arranged with Kari's parents to take their daughter on a little mystery trip the week before the B-Mitzvah. They went to a park and sat down beside the river. *Hazzan* Amy spread a colorful fabric and set upon it a Miriam's cup. This cup is a fairly new ritual item in Jewish life. Moses' sister Miriam was able to find water during the Israelite's travels in the wilderness; her wells are seen as a metaphor for the presence of God, abundance, and women's wisdom as an aspect of the Divine.

The cantor lifted the cup and spoke of her student's strengths, talents, and accomplishments. She asked if there was anything blocking her student's happiness at this time. Kari shared three things, and they made a plan to deal with each.

Hazzan Amy then told Kari that if either of them ever left the congregation, Kari would always be special to her and that she would want to help or hear if a difficult or amazing time should arise in Kari's life, when Kari might not know whom to tell or call. *Hazzan* Amy asked her to try to remain in touch: "E-mail, call me, reach out. My students are very precious to me."

"And," *Hazzan* Amy concluded, "this Miriam's cup is my present for you. Place it on your Shabbat and *seder* table beside the *Kiddush* cup; fill it with spring water and remember that you can always draw from Miriam's cup of abundance, wisdom, and blessing."

"*Hazzan* Amy," asked Kari, "Can I give you a blessing?" And she did.

---

reasons. These two sons of Joseph were the first set of Jewish brothers in Torah who did not fight with each other. They grew up in Egypt and yet maintained a Jewish life despite the forces of persecution and assimilation. They were also grandchildren of the patriarch Jacob and fulfilled the important aphorism: "The issue is not whether you have Jewish children, it is whether you will have Jewish grandchildren."

So long as your parents live, they can bestow these blessings upon you and also expand upon them extemporaneously to make the sentiments more personal. Traditional blessings are not meant to be end points but rather springboards to express the prayer of your heart.

Preparing To Bless The B-Mitzvah Initiate

- You might take the time right now to create a list of the positive qualities of a soon-to-be B-Mitzvah student who is important to you.
- What positive feelings do you have about this person— perhaps pride, admiration, love, joy at your connection, amazement? Take a few minutes to record these feelings.
- You might write these qualities and feelings on a gift card or the border of a picture mounted for framing, carve them into a bowl or *challah* board, or paint them onto a fabric placemat or hanging.
- At just the right presentation moment, perhaps at the party or privately, share these thoughts and feelings. Leave your concerns aside; just let your sense of this person's light shine.
- Consider creating a blessing circle at the reception, where the inner circle of the student's life can be invited to step forward to share their blessings.

Although parents often choose to speak longer and to include some of the journey of raising the B-Mitzvah student, effective brief blessings from guests might sound something like these:

Person One: Dearest Ryan, you have always been a curious person, wondering how things work and where they originate. I bless you to remain curious, to bring your strong mind to uncovering some of the reasons behind things that seem mysterious in life. I bless you with the possibility of even making important discoveries.

Person Two: My good friend Ryan, we are always heading off on bike hikes together. Well, I have a dream that is a blessing: we will bike across Israel or part of America or Europe together one day and always remain the best of friends.

Person Three: Dear Ryan, I know you cut back on soccer practice this year in order to focus on your *Bar Mitzvah* studies. Well, from what I can see, you made the goals you set for yourself for your *Bar Mitzvah*. I bless you to take these skills of life you have claimed for yourself-determination, focus, strategy, practice, and team work—and for you to experience them as an everlasting winner's bouquet of support for your life.

Saying Thank You

Gratitude is one of the most important human emotions. As the B-Mitzvah day nears, it is time to contemplate how to thank those who have been on your B-Mitzvah team during this time of preparation and accomplishment. It helps to start a list early and to keep adding to it. When you stand before those gathered in honor of your transition, take a moment to meet the eyes of those on your list. Let them sense the truth of your gratitude, and then simply state your truth in a loving and diplomatic way. You might go back to your B-Mitzvah mission statement and then be able to fulfill the mitzvah of gratitude, *hakarat ha-tov* by saying something like this:

[Emotions] "Dear family, friends, and teachers: This has been a fantastic year for me. And now here I am, so happy to be surrounded by all the most important people in my life. I thank every one of you for being here with me today.

[Intellect and learning] I learned how to set goals and to create and fulfill objectives in four dimensions—emotional, intellectual, spiritual, and practical—and to accomplish them. I learned so much about how meaningful Judaism is for living and have become so proud to be a capable Jew.

[Spiritual, connections, support] Several people in particular have supported me throughout this process. My parent(s) must come first. You had a vision that my *Bar Mitzvah* could be so much more than I'd ever been exposed to. I feared we would struggle a lot during this process, and instead we are closer than ever; and I feel so appreciated and supported by you. I love you very much and feel very lucky to have such creative, caring parents.

Now those present may not know that I had three *Bar Mitzvah* mentors. Would *Hazzan* Ben please rise? *Hazzan*, you have been so patient with me as I learned the service, and you taught me how to find a note and hold it—it turns out I really can have a good voice. I never knew that. You gave me such a gift with this knowledge. I will never forget you.

Would Erin please rise? I am a very fidgety student and learn best when I'm being physical. Erin has an acting background, and she helped me to study my Torah portion by my becoming each of the characters and walking around acting out their parts and imagining missing lines.

Would Uncle Fred please rise? My Uncle Fred organized a men's circle for me, and we met every six weeks to talk about important things in life. We also had a camping trip together. Because of my mentors, I never felt alone in this process, and I also discovered a lot about myself and Judaism that I like and never knew.

Lots of small and special things have been included in this *Bar Mitzvah* because people took time out to do them. Tante (aunt) Miriam, thank you for the fascinating centerpieces; Grandma Ellen, the kippot you crocheted look so great on everyone; cousins Arnold, Eli, and Kate—you did a mitzvah by making everyone feel welcome in the coatroom, at the gift table, and in the parking lot. And my sister Anna, I will never forget the night you reminded me that some stresses can be rejected, that I could just say no to doing one more passage, and the world wouldn't come to an end.

And finally, I want to thank my rabbi. It was so much fun to see you get excited about all the little extras we put into this *Bar Mitzvah*. Every time I saw your screen name in my e-mail, I knew you had an idea to share too or that you were just checking in on me in the nicest way. My rabbi was the one who found the Yehudah Amichai poem that everyone read at the service today, and I think everyone experienced during the service how special you are.

So thank you everyone. Now let's dance!

Harvesting Memories, Acknowledging Changes

It is Friday night, the week after the B-Mitzvah. Family and close friends are seated at the table about to bless the wine. Someone knocks at the door. Ben and Sara's mom call out: "Who is there?"

"Why it is I, your son, Ben."

"And I, your daughter, Sara, who last week was a girl, but this Shabbat I arrive as a Jewish woman, to help lead the rituals of Shabbat."

"And I, Ben, return a young Jewish man, also ready to help lead the rituals of Shabbat."

All rise from their seats. The parents hurry to open the door. "Come in, dearest ones. Come lead this family in the rituals of *erev* Shabbat."

This adaptation of a Sephardic ritual is one way of continuing the special quality of the B-Mitzvah season, honoring the transition, and continuing to build your memories.

Too often the last step in a B-Mitzvah is the writing of thank-you notes. After having spent so much consciousness in the planning, remember that a conscious process for revisiting your experience is equally valuable.

Some families create a memory book from photos and other memorabilia that have been part of the journey and can help capture the experience. This book can include a few photos along the path of growing up, of studies with tutors and mentors, of excursions to research aspects of the B-Mitzvah, a copy of the *d'var Torah*, blessings given and received, brochures, pressed flowers, pieces of cards received, and other memorabilia. How will you organize your memory book? By the order of events? By special relationships? Or perhaps based on your B-Mitzvah Action Plan (BMAP) list of goals and objectives?

Have fun putting finishing touches to your memory book. Stop by a craft supply store and pick up caption labels that are specially designed for animating photos. This way you can write the names of those in the photos for posterity and also add cute or memorable expressions to make the book more of a story than a gallery. You can use magazines for illustrations, too; crop surprise and other facial emotions and pretty images for borders; clip and apply expressive words of many sizes.

Alternatively, create a website for your B-Mitzvah— include your BMAP, *d'var Torah*, an image of the invitation, photos, and perhaps a video clip. You can even create and send thank-you notes by e-mail to your guests and include a link to the site. If you start the site early in your process, you can build in a family tree zone; here guests can write to send in their photos and comments, view destination maps, and RSVP on-line.

Final Considerations

Are your photos on your computer? Drop relevant ones into your thank-you notes to make them more personal.

Return to the BMAP with a mentor or with your team as a way of integrating your experience more powerfully. Points to cover would include the following:

What about the logistics worked? What didn't? What might you do the same or differently next time there's a family *simcha*?

What emotions have you had during this process? How do you feel now? How do these feelings compare with your expectations? Is there anything you want or need in order to feel complete in relationship to the B-Mitzvah?

What new ideas, concepts, and thoughts came to you because of this process? What has become more clear for you? Do you feel that you met your intellectual goals? What questions have emerged because of this season in your life?

How has your spirit shifted because of this process? Did it help change your relationship to prayer, God, and Torah? Did you accomplish the spiritual goals you set? Were the qualities of intimacy, joy, connection, philanthropy, and peoplehood present in ways that you'd hoped for?

Mazel tov to everyone on the B-Mitzvah team—you have accomplished so much!

This book has provided a bumper crop of ideas for creating a more meaningful and memorable B-Mitzvah. We've also been through a planning process together—establishing emotional, intellectual, and spiritual goals and formulating excellent logistics to support those goals. Every step of the path of preparation for B-Mitzvah has had a chapter full of creative educational, spiritual, and practical guidance. Your ability to enjoy this precious time rather than feeling stressed out, to delight in this experience for yourself, friends, and family have been our goals. May you be blessed with a life rich in joyful and fulfilling Jewishing for many, many years to come!

Visit Bmitzvah.org to ask questions of the author, Rabbi Goldie Milgram, and share the fruits of your experience with others. Here you will also find information about local B-Mitzvah Family Adventure Workshops for enhancing and advancing the youth and adult B-Mitzvah experience in your community, as well as explore our two non-profit websites that offer hundreds of regularly-updated ideas, bibliography, resources and programs for a more meaningful and memorable Bar or Bat Mitzvah and spiritually fulfilling Jewish life.

Bmitzvah.org
ReclaimingJudaism.org

Innovative Programs, Books & Resources for Meaningful Jewish Living

Glossary
Transliterations And Translations

All terms interpreted here are Hebrew unless otherwise indicated. There is no "ch" sound, as in the word "change," in Hebrew or Yiddish. The letter combination "ch," when used here, is meant to be pronounced gutturally, as "kh."

adon (ah-dohn) Standard translation is "Lord"; mystical meaning is from its root (eh-den), meaning "windowsill" or "threshold" as a metaphorical name for God.

afikoman (ah-fee-koe-mahn) During the Passover evening ritual known as a *seder*, a sheet of matzah is broken in half and hidden. As the ritual ends, the youngest present search for it, and only when they have found it and so have taken a personal role in supporting the ritual process can the *seder*'s final ritual prayers be recited.

ahavah (ah-hah-vah) Love, one of the core principles of Judaism, *ahavat* (ah-hah-vaht) Love of.

Aleynu (ah-ley-noo) "On us"—the name and first word of almost the last prayer of every Jewish service. Its essence is that we take "on us" responsibility for participating in the repair and renewal of the world in terms of social justice, the environment, peace, and more; during the prayer we bow in acknowledgment of the melech—the innate and amazing design and self-governance of creation and our limited role within it.

aliyah (ah-lee-yah; aliyot [pi] ah-lee-ote) Literally "going up"—a term used two ways: (1) for going up to the Torah to witness it being read and (2) for fulfilling the mitzvah of moving to Israel.

amidah (ah-mee-dah) Literally "standing"—the prayer sequence midway through services that includes time for silently finding the prayer of your heart.

aron (ah-rone) Ark, as in the cabinet where a Torah is kept.

atarah (ah-tah-rah) Decorative collar of a *tallit* (prayer shawl), which often has embroidered upon it the blessing for putting it on.

av (ahv) Father; short form of the formal Hebrew word for father (abba).

avelim (ah-vey-lim) Mourners.

b'derech (b'deh-rekh) Literally "on the road"; can mean "in the way of" or in the "manner of," as in *b'derech nashim*, in the "way of women."

b'tzelem (b'tzeh-lem) In the image of; humans are described in Genesis as having been created "in the image of God.

baal (bah-ahl) Master, as in someone who has mastered a skill or as in head of household or kingdom.

baalei (bah-ah-ley) Masters of.

badhan (bahd-han; badhanim (pl) bahd-hah-nim) Yiddish for party entertainers who clown around—jugglers, stand-up comedians, and such.

bat (baht) Daughter.

bayit (bah-yeet) House or housing, as in the casing for something, such as the little black boxes that encase small handwritten scrolls of specific verses from the Torah.

bedikat (b'dee-kaht) Checking of, examination of; as in *bedikat chametz*—checking for crumbs in rooms being made kosher for Passover by removing anything that was made from or has come in contact with leavening.

ben (behn) Son.

berachah (b'rah-khah; berachot (pl) b'rah-khot) Blessing—from the word family *berech* "knee" and *b'reychah* "pond"; making a blessing is meant to invoke a sense of bending one's knee before the pond of life, which is full of blessings.

bereshit (b'rey-sheet; often seen in Ashkenazi form, bereshis) "In the beginning"; also the Hebrew name for first book of Genesis, the first chapter of the Torah.

bimah (bee-mah) Podium, stage, raised platform for a religious service.

bris (bris, Ashkenazic and folk; brit (breet), Sephardic and modern Hebrew) Covenant, often seen in association with the phrase *brit milah*, covenant of circumcision.

challah; challot (pl) (khah-lah, sometimes affectionately called khallie) Braided Sabbath egg bread.

chametz (khah-meytz; Yiddish, khuh-metz) Foods made with leavening or prepared before Passover in a facility not made ready for Passover.

chaya (kha-ya) Vitality, one of the five levels of soul, *chayyim* (kha-yim) Life.

cheshbon (khesh-bohn) Check or bill in a restaurant, or practice of doing a *cheshbon ha-nefesh*, accounting of one's soul.

cholim (khoe-lim) Those who are ill.

Chumash (Khu-mahsh) Five Books of Moses.

daat (dah-aht) Knowledge.

derasha (d'rah-shah) Explanation of something in the Torah that is based on an enquiry that deepens what it might mean; Israeli term for a *d'var Torah*.

dertzeylerin (dehr-tzey-lehr-in) Yiddish term for storyteller.

divrei (div-ray) Words of, or interpretations of; possessive form of *d'var*.

drash (drahsh) Short for *derasha*.

d'var (d'vahr) A word or thing, as in a *d'var Torah*, a "word of Torah," meaning a teaching about something in the Torah given at services, at a meal, or any meeting or gathering.

echad (ekhad) One.

ehden (eh-den) Windowsill or threshold; root of *Adonai*—"Lord."

ehyeh imach (Eh-heh im-makh) Quote from Torah; when asked at the burning bush by Moses what name God wishes to be known by, the answer is these words meaning, "I Will Be is with you."

eirastich li (Ey-rahsh-tikh lee) I betroth/commit myself.

eitz (eytz) Tree, as in the *eitz chayyim*, Tree of Life; metaphorical name for the Torah, for one of two named trees in the Garden of Eden, for the wooden rollers upon which a Torah scroll is mounted, and for a meditation practice and model of the Kabbalists.

ekev (Ey-kehv) Name of one of the fifty-four Torah portions; root of Jacob's Hebrew name, Yaakov, meaning heel.

elohim (Eh-loe-him) First term for God given in the Torah.

em (ehm) Mother.

erev (eh-rehv) Evening.

ezrat (ehz-raht) Helper of.

farrible (fah-ree-ble or fur-ree-ble) Yiddish term for when there is a relationship problem between two or more people.

gemilut (g'mee-lute) Deeds of, as in *gemilut hassadim*, deeds of loving-kindness.

genivat (g'nee-vaht) Theft of, as in the mitzvah of not offering faulty advertising, which is termed *genivat daat*, "theft of awareness or knowledge."

geniza (g'nee-za) Storage/burial place for worn-out and no longer useful religious documents, including photocopies, which receive special treatment because the most sacred Hebrew name of God is written upon them. From the root *ganuz*, "hidden," as Judaism believes the full essence of God is inaccessible to humankind.

gevurah (g'voo-rah) Strength; also the qualities of strength and healthy boundaries, as represented by one of the ten *sefirot*—energetic points of special qualities that comprise the Kabbalists' Tree of Life practice.

gragger (grah-gr) Noise-making device used to drown out the name of the villain Haman during the reading of the Book of Esther on Purim.

guf (goof) Body.

hachnassat (hakh-nah-saht) Entry of, as in *hachnassat orchim*, warm and maximally accommodating welcome for arriving guests, which is a sacred duty (mitzvah) in Judaism.

hadarta (hah-dahr-tah) Glorying, as in honoring senior adults.

haftorah (Haf-toe-rah, folk; haf-tah-rah, modern Hebrew) Prophetic reading for a given week that is chanted after the Torah portion at Sabbath morning services.

hamsa (hahm-suh) Hand-shape Middle-Eastern symbol for luck.

hassadim (hah-sah-dim) Loving-kindnesses, as in *gemilut hassadim*, deeds of loving-kindness.

havdalah (Hahv-dah-lah) Separation or distinction; name for the closing ritual of the Sabbath, held Saturday evening when three stars become visible or would be visible if the weather would allow.

havurah (hah-voo-rah; havurot (pl) hah-vue-rote) Friendship, a term for relatively small Jewish groups where members meet to study or pray together. These often have a less formal institutional framework than synagogues, although some are subgroups within existing synagogues formed to allow for greater intimacy, creativity, and participation.

hazzan (hah-zahn) Cantor—one specially ordained in the rituals of Jewish sacred music.

hessed (heh-sehd) Loving-kindness; also one of the ten qualities in the Tree of Life practice of the Kabbalists.

hevdalim (hev-dah-lim) Distinctions, differences.

hevruta (hev-roo-tah) A friend with whom one studies Torah regularly.

hiddur (hee-door) Embroider, beautify, as in *hiddur* mitzvah, elaboration of a mitzvah-like act of consciousness or religious object to make it more beautiful.

hitbodedut (hit-boe-deh-dute; often heard in Ashkenazi/Hassidic pronunciation, his-bo-de-dus) Category of meditation practices for making yourself alone with God.

hod (hoed) One of the ten qualities of the sephirot in the Kabbalists' Tree of Life practice, where one allows for incubation and development of an idea, plan, intention, hope.

hubbatzin (huh-buh-tzin) Yiddish/English term coined in 1988 by Rabbi Goldie Milgram for the male life-partner of a rabbi, paralleling *rebbetzin*, the term for a female life-partner of a rabbi.

kaballah (kah-bah-lah) Receiving—a general term referring to the substantial body of Jewish mystical knowledge and practices.

kaddish (kah-dish) Aramaic prayer affirming awe at life, revealed in the many evolving manifestations of God in the process of creation and ends with a prayer for peace; said in several forms during religious services and so helps link discrete sections of the service. At times mourners rise to recite a specific version of this prayer for up to a year after the death of a first-degree family member; another form is recited during services to memorialize the many generations of Torah scholars.

kashrut (kash-rute; Ashkenazi, kash-rus) The practice of keeping kosher, meaning that animals are slaughtered with consciousness of a life being taken and of how they were raised; specific animals and fishes are not permitted; blood is never eaten and is drained out before cooking and discarded; milk is never eaten with meat. For major events caterers hire a *mashgiach*, a specialist in *kashrut* supervision, to handle details.

kattan (kah-than) Small, as in a *tallit kattan*, a light-weight four-cornered garment some Jews wear under their clothes as a reminder to live a mitzvah-centered life.

kayam (kah-yahm) Existence.

kehillah (k'hee-luh; kehillot (pl) kuh-hee-lote) Community.

kibbud (kee-bude) Honor, as in *kibbud av v'em*, honoring one's father and mother.

kiddushin (kee-doo-sheen) Name for one of the books of the Talmud and term for the Jewish marriage ritual, based on its root word, *kiddush*, or holiness.

kippah (key-pah; kippot (pl) key-pote) Scull cap—a ritual headcovering worn for prayer, ritual, and study, and by some all day (except when in the shower or swimming); often known by the Greek term *yarmulke*.

klezmorim (klehz-mohr-im) Players of Eastern European genre known as Klezmer music, which is alternatively joyful and sad, with themes reflecting daily life, joys, and struggles; many joyful, easy-to-dance-to tunes.

kodesh (koe-desh) Holiness.

kol (kawl) All.

lashon (lah-shone) Language.

l'fanecha (l'fah-neh-kha) Before you.

l'hanee-ach (l'hah-nee-akh) To put at rest or at ease; also part of the blessing for putting on *tefillin*.

l'hitatef (l'hit-ah-tef) To wrap, as in to wrap yourself in a prayer shawl.

ma-ah-chil (ma-ah-khil) Feeding, as in the mitzvah of maachil r'eyvim, feeding those who are hungry.

maggid (mah-geed; maggidim (pl) mah-gi-deem) Sacred story teller.

malchut (mahl-khute) Domain or kingdom of; also one of the ten sephirot of the Tree of Life practice of the Kabbalists that completes their holographic understanding of the universe.

melech (meh-lekh) King, a metaphor for God as the governing principle of the universe, as in *melech ha-olam*.

Menachot (Meh-nah-khot) Book/Tractate of the Talmud concerning discussion and rules about Temple meal offerings, *tzitzit* (fringes), and *tallit* (prayer shawl).

menorah (m'noh-rah) Candelabra that originally appeared in the wilderness sanctuary, Mishkan, with seven branches; now appears in homes on Hanukkah with nine branches so as to be a memorial honoring the Maccabbees' reclaiming of the Temple.

migba-at (mig-bah-aht) Specialized turban or hat worn by the high priest.

min (mihn) From, or type of.

minyan (min-yahn) Collective term for the ten individuals required to begin a religious service.

mitznefet (meetz-neh-fet) Turban worn by priests described in the Torah.

mitzvah (meetz-vah; mitz-vah, folk pronunciation) Commandment; sacred act done with consciousness.

modah (moe-dah [f]; modeh [m] moe-deh) Praising.

nachas (nah-khas) Yiddish for pleasure derived from how one's students, children, or grandchildren live their lives.

nashim (nah-shim) Women.

nedivat (n'dee-vaht) Generosity of, as in *nedivat lev*, generosity that comes from the heart.

neechum (nee-khum) Comfort, as in *neechum aveileem*, comforting mourners by visiting them, bringing them provisions, and listening.

nefesh (neh-fesh) A soul.

neshamah (n'shah-mah) Another of five terms for the soul,

olam (oh-lahm) World, universe, eternity.

omer (oh-mehr) Measure of grain brought as an offering to the temple each of the days between Passover and Shavuot; today we count each of those days as a spiritual practice called counting the *omer*— working on specific qualities of character assigned for reflection on each of the days.

oneg (oh-nehg) Pleasure; also the term for serving a light meal or sweets after services for the pleasure of guests and in honor of Shabbat.

or (ohr) Light.

orchim (ohr-khim) Guests.

parsha (pahr-shah) Each of the fifty-four Torah portions is called a *parsha*.

parshat (pahr-shaht; parshiot (pl) pahr-shee-ote) Portion of; possessive form that appears when naming a portion, for example *parshat Lech L'cha.*

pikuach (pee-koo-akh) Save, as in *pikuach nefesh*—a major mitzvah, that of saving a life (soul).

p'nai (p'ney) Faces of, as in *p'nai* Shabbat—faces of Shabbat or the qualities we welcome within and among ourselves that are the true nature of Shabbat as a spiritual practice.

p'shat (p'shaht) Simple, basic understanding of a text.

rachamim (rah-kha-mim) Compassion, from root *rechem*, meaning womb.

remez (reh-mehz) Hint; also a level of interpretation that goes beyond the obvious, based upon how a word can point to another level of realization.

r'evim (r'ey-vim) Those who are hungry, as in poor and starving.

ruach (rue-akh) Breath, wind, spirit; one of the terms for the five levels of soul.

seder (seh-der, modern Hebrew; sey-dehr, folk) Order; name of the table ritual held at Passover.

sefirot (seh-fee-rote) In the Kabbalists' Tree of Life practice there are points of meaning that have qualities we can refine in ourselves; each is called a *s'firah*, from the same root as Shapiro and sapphire, with the root meaning nice.

seudah (s'oo-dah) A meal.

Shabbat (shah-baht, modern Hebrew; shah-bos, folk) Resting, Sabbath; from the verb in Genesis, *vayishbote*—and (God) rested.

Shaddai (shah-dye) Hills, breasts; metaphorical name for God as nurturing.

shaliach (shah-lee-akh) Messenger sent with a task on behalf of someone.

Shechinah (Sheh-khee-nah) Aspect of God as presence, that is, the energy, flow, and intimacy of creation. Feminine aspect of God for some periods of Jewish interpretation.

shel (shell) Of.

rosh (roesh) Head, as in the *tefillin* that is *shel rosh*, of the head, or Rosh HaShannah, the Head of the Year, the Jewish New Year.

shamati (shah-mah-ti) I've heard, have listened deeply.

shelishit (sh'lee-sheet) Third, as in *seudah shelishit*, third and final meal of the Sabbath.

shema (sh'mah) Hear! Listen! Major prayer in services, from Deuteronomy; found in mezuzah and *tefillin* and recited upon going to sleep.

shevuim (sh'voo-im) Captives, as in the mitzvah of *pidyon shevuim*, redeeming captives (for example, via Amnesty International).

shiflut (shee-flute) Humility.

shirah (shee-rah) Song.

shiva (shiv-uh) Period of seven days of intensive mourning after the funeral of an immediate relative; visitors sit with you while you stay home, deeply honoring the one who has passed and taking time to integrate the loss.

shmirat (shmeer-aht) Watching of, as in *shmirat ha-guf*, taking care of your body.

shomer (show-mehr [m]; *shomeret* [f] show-meh-ret) One who watches over or is observant of the mitzvot; a friend who helps someone having a religious ceremony by being a volunteer personal attendant for the day of the ritual.

Shulchan Aruch (shule-khan ah-rukh) Authoritative law code summarizing major principles up to 1560 C.E., then expanded in 1570.

siddur (see-door) Prayer book.

simcha (sim-kha) Celebration for a major life-cycle event or accomplishment such as graduating from school or having a B-Mitzvah; root word *simcha* means "happiness."

smichah (smee-khah) Ordination as a rabbi or cantor.

Sukkot (soo-kote, Sephardi and modem Hebrew; suk-kos, Ashkenazi) Harvest holiday where for a week we take meals outdoors in fragile huts appreciating nature and hosting guests.

ta'amode (tah-ah-mode) Rise! Feminine command form for inviting someone to rise and come up to the Torah as a witness to the reading of the sacred story.

ta-ir (tah-eer) Will be lit, as in a flame or light.

tallit (tah-leet; *tallitot* [pi] tah-lee-tote) Prayer shawl(s) with fringes worn for praying and leading services, also for burial and as a daily *tallit kattan*; worn under clothes; all have fringes to remind one to live a mitzvah-centered life.

teefrosh (tee-froesh) Separate yourself, as in *al teefrosh min ha-tzibur*, "don't separate yourself from the community."

tefillin (t'fee-leen, modem Hebrew; t'fill-in, folk) Morning meditation practice. Done with a ritual set of straps, each with an attached box holding sections of handwritten Torah text; worn on the arm and head, connecting head and heart.

teraphim (t'rah-fim) Term that appears so infrequently in the Bible that scholars cannot definitively say what it means; some say idols; others conjecture it is an astronomy tool and more.

terumah (t'rue-mah) Temple offering brought freely; described in a Torah portion by the same name.

teshuvah (t'shoo-vah) Mitzvah of transforming negative energy in a relationship (between you and someone, yourself and God, yourself and yourself) to a better place so healing and forgiveness can begin to happen.

tiferet (teef-eh-reht) Compassionate justice, the heart place in the system of ten sephirot.

tikkun (tee-kuhn) Repair and renewal, as in *tikkun olam*—the mitzvah of social justice and social action for people and the planet.

Torah (Toh-rah, Toe-ruh, folk pronunciation) Five Books of Moses, handwritten on a scroll by a scribe in special Hebrew calligraphy.

tummler (tuhm-lr) Yiddish for a ceremonial leader at a party who really knows how to get everyone joyfully involved.

tzaar (tzah-ahr) Pain, suffering; *tzurris* in Yiddish.

tzedakah (tz'dah-kah) Equitable distribution of resources, sometimes called charity.

tzibbur (tzee-bohr) Congregation, as in *k'vod ha-tzibur*, deciding what is appropriate in order to honor the values of a community.

tzion (tzee-yone) The Promised Land, Zion, Israel.

tzitzit (tzih-tziht, modern Hebrew; tzih-tzis, Ashkenazi pronunciation) Fringes on the four corners of a prayer shawl, *tallit*.

v' And.

v'tzeevanu (v'tzee-vah-nu) Commanded us.

ya'amode (Yah-ah-mode) Arise! As in being called to the covenantal honor of witnessing the Torah reading; masculine form.

yad (yahd) Hand; also the shape of and term for the pointer used by the Torah reader so as not to smear the letters with the oils in one's hand.

yadat (yah-daht) You will know.

yarmulke (yahr-muhl-kuh) Greek for skullcap or *kippah*, ritual cover for one's head during services, blessings, and, for some, life.

yechidah (y'khee-dah) Complete awareness of unity with All Being, one of the five levels of soul.

yesod (y'sode) Foundation. One of the ten sephirot of the Kabbalists associated with generative life-force energy.

YHVH Unpronounceable as a word or name, this series of Hebrew letters Yud Hey Vav Hey—known as the tetragrammaton—is the sacred name of God made of all tenses of the verb "to be."

yizkor (yeez-kore; yiz-kr, folk) Will be remembered; service offered on several holidays when one is supported in recalling those close who have died and those who have died helping our people survive.

zaken (zah-ken) Elder.

Acknowledgments

This work was made possible by the encouragement and support of Dr. Ruth Durchslag and the Nathan Cummings Foundation. I am also very grateful to Arthur Kurzweil and Jossey-Bass, a Wiley Imprint, for being the first to support and publish this body of my research and writing. The guidance and experiences described herein derive from years of doctoral research during which unflagging interest, support, and encouragement were freely given by the board members of P'nai Yachadut—Reclaiming Judaism, as well as a doctoral advisory team and manuscript readers: Adam and Mark Beitman, Sara and Fred Harwin, Lynn Hazan, Iva Kauffman, Karen Stuck Mortensen, Dr. George McClain, Sue Shapiro, David Rifkin, Janice Rubin, Jacke Schroeder, Nancy Sher, Dr. Sharon Ufberg, Ellen Weaver, and Rabbi Shohama Wiener and Sarah Shadowitz.

The methods offered herein were tested in a wide variety of denominational contexts, as well as contexts of balanced and respectful pluralism. Vocal champions of the importance of reframing *Bar/Bat Mitzvah* (B-Mitzvah) as a process full of mentoring, meaning, and spirituality include not only those already listed, but also those who have been consulted and those who help to develop supportive contexts for this work to fully manifest throughout Jewish life. Heartfelt appreciation for this also goes to Shoshana Bricklin, Liz Cutler, Abby Pitkowsky, *Hazzan* Ed Roffman, Rabbi Steven Rubenstein, Chana Silberstein, and Dr. Helene Tigay.

My perspective in doing this work has been deeply shaped by decades of dedicated teachers and mentors. Particularly in relationship to *Bar/Bat Mitzvah* preparation, I am very grateful for the seeds of creativity planted in me by many members of the Jewish clergy: Robert Layman, who facilitated my *Bat Mitzvah* in 1968; Zalman Schachter-Shalomi and David Wolfe-Blank z"l, who created meaningful prayer maps and applied the Kabbalist's *Eitz Chayyim* and Four Worlds models to Jewish practice; Nancy Fuchs-Kreimer and Linda Holtzman, who expanded rabbinical training by introducing ways of understanding life as a spiritual journey; Simcha Paull Raphael and Geela Rayzl Raphael who modeled applications of the personal *kehillah* model; Robert Esformes, Jack Kessler, and Neil Schwartz, who revealed how cantillation of sacred text can be a force for meaning.

My boundless appreciation also goes to Rabbis Shefa Gold, Marcia Prager, Jeff Roth, and Shawn Zevit; Drs. Peter Pitzele, Gene Gendlin, Laura Vidmar, and Shlomo Bardin z"l; members of Achiot Or; and Alan Ganapol. Their remarkable experiential methods help bring so many students more fully into a life deeply and joyfully lived through a Jewish spiritual lens.

This work has also been shaped by hundreds of questions and letters that students and parents passionately seeking to deepen their B-Mitzvah experience have sent to the author at Bmitzvah.org.

The editorial guidance of Alan Rinzler, Arthur Kurzweil, Andrea Flint, and Genevieve Duboscq have been invaluable in this process. And to Anne Edelstein, my literary agent, please know that your depth of commitment and engagement has made all the difference.

Ultimately, a great deal of appreciation is due my beloved *hubbatzin*, Barry Bub, who patiently and creatively made this period of intensive effort possible through his loving attention to the details of daily living and profound commitment to the importance of this work.

Index

A

Aaron, High Priest, brother of
    Moses
Abraham, 21, 119, 142-143
Adonai, 108
Agunot, 140
AIDS, d'var Torah
Aliyah to the Torah, 69, 184
    family, 34
    group, 34
Amidah, (See Prayer)
Ancestors, 20
Animals, 69
Angel(s), 143
Ark, *aron*, (See Symbols)
Art. making gifts, 199-201
    Incorporating in d'var Torah,
    70
Ashkenaz(ic)(im), 119

B

Bar and bat mitzvah,
    b'nei mitzvah (pl), ages for, 22,
    28
    adult 28
    BMAP (action plan), see
    BMAP blessing, 22, 42-43
    celebration, (See Celebration)
    cross-cultural comparison 22-
    28, 37
    date, selection considerations
    for ritual, 26
    history and evolution, 21, 42
    in Israel, 184
    invitations, 47
    party, (See Celebration), 47
    retreats, 183
    team, inner-circle, 49
    universal elements, 26-27

baruch sheh petarani, (See Blessings)

b'derech nashim, 40

b'tzelem Elohim, 172

Bible, (See Torah)

Bilhah, 140

Blessing(s), brachot, 27, 130
    bar mitzvah blessing, traditional baruch sheh petarani, 22
    shehecheyanu, 22
    kiss, first, 44
    mentor(s), mentoring, tutoring, 25, 44, 47
    parental blessing, guide to writing, 203-4
    physical change, 25, 44
    tallit, tallis, prayer shawl, 47, 104-105
    tefillin, 112-113

BMAP (action plan), 31-49
    mission statement, 19, 46-50, 177, 204
    overview, 31
    motional goals and objectives, 32-38
    intellectual goals and objectives, 39-41, 79-114
    reviewing six months after B-Mitzvah, 207
    spiritual goals and objectives, 41-44
    logistical, physical goals and objectives, 40, 45-49

Body, (See Mitzvah, shmirat ha-guf), respect and caring for body, 74, 159

voice and vocal coach(ing), 74

Boundaries, 52, 60, clothing, 150

Broken tablets, 132

Budget(ing), 36

C

Cake, 35

Caleb, 134

Calendar, Hebrew, Jewish, date selection considerations, 26

Candles, Candle-lighting, 21, 35, 100
    Havdalah, 35
    metaphor, 135

Cantors (See Hazzan)

Celebration, 171-194
    artists, 172-3
    caterer, 176
    centerpieces, 193
    dance, 172
    family, 32, 176
    greening your celebration, 180
    guests, selecting, 38
    lodging, 179
    roles for, 182
    issues re inviting whole class, 190
    henna, 173
    humorists, badhanim, 172
    invittations, 178-179, 181
    music, songs (See Music)
    cross-cultural, 37, 173
    photography, 37, 186
    planning, 37
    reception, 32

cabaret, salon, 39
potluck, 183
major, 171-194
skits, 185
themes, 187-192
tummler, 185
Challah, 100
Change, documenting and reflecting on personal change, 61-66, 73,
Children, 139, 155
Clergy, 23
COEJL, 68
Cost, (See Budget)

D

Dan, 140
Date, for ritual, selection considerations, 26
Death, 24
Developmental support, 651-76
learning styles, 52-55
personality, 56, 60-61
talents and Skills, 57-59
life as a story, spiritual journey, 61-66
personal *kehillah*, support group, 71-74
Dinah, 39, 44
Difference, diversity, 32
Disabilities, (See Special Needs)
Divorce, 69
Donations (see Tzedakah, opportunities)
Dream, 137

Dress, 150
D'var Torah, 117-152
characters and objects 131-132
characteristics of a memorable d'var, 131, 144
delivery (See Public Speaking), methods for creating,
bibliodrama, 138-141
commentaries, 145-148
culture and time, 145
elements, identifying key ones, 124
midrash-style, 138-141
noticing time periods of text, 124
outline of the parsha, 125-127
reactions to the text, 129-130
relating to current events, 135-135, 141
scripting the parsha, 127-128
finding symbols and metaphors, 135-137
welcoming awareness, revelation, 141-143
writing letter to a character or object, 132
purpose, 118

E

Eitz Chayyim, Tree of Life, 70,
Emotion(s)(al), 135, 32
goals (See BMAP)
Ephraim, 201
Esau, 33
Ethiopian Jews, 199

F

Family,
    divorce, 69
    support at the reception (See
    Celebration)
    remarriage, 69
    tree, family tree creation, 34
    twins, 32
Father, fathering, 21-22
Federation, Jewish, 83
Focusing, 92-93
Friendship, inner-circle, minyan
    of your life, 94-95, 159

G

Garden of Eden, *gan eden*, 70
Gardner, Howard, 53
Gender, 21
Genealogy, 191
Germany, 39
Gift(s),
    activities as gifts, 199
    from family and legacy, heri-
    tage, 196-200
God,
    connecting, connection, expe-
    riences, 26, 93, 159, 192
    ehyeh asher ehyeh, I am becom-
    ing what I am becoming, 62
    hitbodedut, practice for being
    alone with God, Jacob en-
    countering God, interpreta-
    tion, names of God, *ehyeh*, 62
    shelter, 67

Golden calf, 192
Grandparent(s)(ing), 37, 39, 42,
    47, 164, 188, 198-199
Gratitude, 204-205
Guests (See Celebration)

H

Hagar, 142-143
Hamsa, 39, 192
Havdallah, 178, 189
Hazan, cantor, 202
Hebrew, why meaningful, 90
Hevrutah guide, 133
Hibodedut, hisbodedus, 86-87
Hiddur mitzvah, 22, 193
History,
    B-Mitzvah, 21, 42
    time periods covered by the
    five Biblical books, 124
Holidays, 20
Holocaust, 51, 188
Homelessness, 167, 169
Humility, *shiflut*, 119

I

Initiation Rites, 19-28
    Comparative (See Bar/Bat
    Mitzvah)
Intellect(ual) goals,
    selection and implementa-
    tion, 39-49
    equal rights, 39
Isaac, 126, 142-143
Ishmael, 127

J

Jacob, 33, 40, 119, 138, 202
Jacob's ladder, 135
Joshua, 134
Joshua 2:1-24
Journey, 35
Justice, 20, 41, 46, 112, 123, 140, 153-154, 160-161, 165

K

Kabbalah, 70
    seven sefirot as used for tefillin, 111-112
Kaddish, 34
    remembering relatives at service or ritual, (See Memorial)
Kallah,
    Shabbat bride, 98
Kehillah, (See Community, building)
Keturah, 126
Kiddush, 100, cup, 202
Kinesthetic learning, 53-55
King David, 33, 119
Kippah, kippot, skullcap, yarmulke, 104-108
Kohelet, 33

L

Laban, Lavan, 40, 138
Leah, 33, 138-140, 201
Learning styles, 53-55

Levi, 139
Listening, 73

M

Maccabiah, 188
Marriage, 24
Martial Arts, 58
Mask(s), 23-4
Meditation, Jewish, 109
Melech, king as metaphor, 99
Memorial(ize), 27, 34, 89, 156, 164
Men, male, masculine, 43, 136
Menashe, 201
Mentor(s), mentoring, 24, 32, 198
    guide to selecting, 146, 168
Metaphor, 35, 99, 118, 128, 135-137, 188-190
Mezuzah, 108-109, 137
Midian(ites), 145
Midrash, 138-141
Minyan, as metaphor, 181
Miriam, 129-130
Miriam's Cup ritual, 202
Mishkan, tabernacle, 70, 217
Mission statement
Mistakes, 36
Mitzvah, mitzvot, 20
    goals, 159-165
    thirteen mitzvah study-plan, 162-164
    ahavat tzion, Israel, love and care, 157, 164
    al tifrosh min ha-tzee-bohr,

minyan, creating community, 158, 164

bal tash-hit , caring for the environment, 156

ezrat cholim, and bikkur cholim, helping those who are ill, visiting them, 154-156

gemillut hassadim, deeds of loving-kindness, 164, 166

genivat da'at, refrain from deception, 157

hachnassat orchim, hosting guests, 157

hadlakat neirot, menorah, candle-lighting, 79-80, 100, 158, 163 (Also see Candle-lighting)

hakarat ha-tov, gratitude, 204-205

heshbon ha-nefesh, accounting of the soul, 157

hiddur mitzvah, beautifying a mitzvah, 22, 193

kashrut, separating milk and meat, conscious eating, 157

kibbud av v'em, honoring parents, 157

leyshev ba-sukkah, sukkah, sitting in, 67, 79, 157

limmud Torah, Torah study, (See Study, also D'var Torah)

ma-ah-chil r'evim, feeding the hungry, 156

mezuzah, marking doorways for listening and loving, 157, 164

neechum aveylim, mourners, support for, 157

pidyon sh'vuim, redeeming captives, 156

pikuach nefesh, saving a life, 157

shalom bayit, peace in the home, 156

shmirat ha-guf, caring for your body, 156

shmirat lashon, refrain from gossip and slander, 156

shmirat Shabbat, keeping the Sabbath day, 79-80, 98-102, 158

tefillah, prayer, (See Prayer)

teshuvah, healing and renewing relationships, (See Teshuvah)

tzaar baalei chayyim, preventing cruelty to animals, 69, 156

tzedek tirdof, pursue justice (See Justice)

tzedekah, charity, philanthropy, (See Tzedakah)

v'hadarta p'nei zaken, honoring elders, 156

yizkor, remembering those who have died, (See Memorial)

zeicher yetziat mitzrayim, seder, freedom, coming out of Egypt, 79-80

Mitzvah project ideas, 154-170, 190

Mitzvnefet, 106
Moses, Moshe, 33, 129-130, 132, 145
Music,
    composition for d'var Torah, 31
    function throughout Bar/Bat Mitzvah, 23
    song(s) cited, Hevdalim, 35
Mysticism, 70

N

Nachman of Breslov, Bratslav, 43, 87
Naftali, 140
Name(s) Jewish, Hebrew, Yiddish,
    finding, choosing, 95-98
    Leah naming her children, 139-140
    of God, (See God)
Nature, 43, 159
Native American, First Peoples, 23-27

O

Organ donation,
    awareness raising as theme and mitzvah project, 190

P

Pachi, 23-28
Parsha(t), see Torah portion
Party (see celebration)

Personality, 56
Pets, 68
Philanthropy (See Tzedakah, opportunities)
Polygamy, 119
Pomegranate(s), 85, 144
Prayer(s),
    tefillah, (See Services)
    map of prayer service, 90-91
    l'cha dodi, 98-99
    modeh, modah ani, 166,
    psalms, 136
    personal, from the heart, 92, 94
    shema, 99, 137
    vision quest, *hitbodedut*, 86-87
Prayer Shawl (See Tallit, tallis)
Presents (See Gifts)
Promises, keeping, 22
Puberty, 24
Public speaking, 33-4, 44, 148-150

Q

R

Rabbi, 23
Rachel, 33, 201
Rashi, 148
Rebecca, 126, 201
Rebellious teenager, 119
Reuben, 139
Ritual(s),
    innovative blessing ritual for while putting fringes on *tallit*, 105

returning home after
B-mitzvah, 206
creating a personal kehillah,
71-74
Rock, Rock of Ages, 136, metaphor, 136
Role modeling, 33
Rosenbloom, Deborah, 184

S

Sabbath. (See Mitzvot)
Sacrifice, sacrificial system, 119,
191
Sarah, 142-143, 201
Seudah shel mitzvah, (See Celebration)
Shechem, 140
Sephardi(c), Sephardim, Sefardi(c),
Sefardim, 39, 173
Service,
creating booklet, 88-90
map, order of , 91
Shabbat ritual, symbols,
prayers, 98-115
tallit, tallis, kippah, yarmulke
customs, 107-108
options for which and when
to hold, 178
Shabbat, (See Mitzvot)
Shaman(ic), 23-28
Shema (See Prayer)
Shiflut, humility, 119
Shimon, 139
Shofar, 79-80
Shomer(et), 182

Siblings, 33, (also see Twins)
Siddur(im),
prayerbook(s), 88-89
map of service outline, 91
understanding the prayers,
90-92, 88-115
Skills, 56-60
Creating prayer service and
booklet, 88-106
listening, 73
reading Torah, (See leyning)
vocal quality and coaching, 74
Song(s), (See Music)
Soul, five levels, 76
Special Needs, 123
Speech, (See d'var Torah)
public speaking, 34-5
Spies, 134
Stories,
Finding Buried Treasure, 110
Missing Mitzvah Feathers,
154-155
The Shaman, The Bar Mitzvah Student and The Rabbi,
23-24
When Imperfection Strikes,
192
The Silver Ring, 196
Miriam's Cup, 202,
Strangers, 159
Study,
plan, 20, 79-115
questions, 82
PARDES method, 144
with a partner, hevruta guide,
133

Sukkah, sukkot, sukkos, 67, 69
Symbol(s)(ism),
    ark, aron, 84-86
    bimah, reading platform/
    stand, 84-86
    rainbow, 192
    breast plate, 84-6
    Torah crown and bells, 84-86
    Torah cover, 84-86
    white, color of transforma-
    tion, 100
    wooden rollers, eitz hayyim,
    84-86
    yad, pointer, 84-86

T

Talents,
    applying during rite of pas-
    sage, 56-59
Tallit, tallis, 47, 92-93, 198-200
Tefillah(ot), prayer(s), (see Prayer)
Tefillin,
    how to put on, 111-113
    meditation 112-113
    story, Finding Buried Trea-
    sure, 10
Teraphim, 40
Teshuvah, repair of relationships,
    143, 163
Text study (See Hevrutah)
Thank you, (See Gratitude)
Torah, 69
    chanting, (See Leyning)
    interpretation, (See D'var
    Torah)

ritual of passing the Torah
through the generations present, 34
outlining a Torah portion,
125-127
Portion(s), elements within
the parsha/text, 124
deriving themes for throughout B-mitzvah, finding match
for a given date or birthday,
120-122
list of with verses, 121
interpretation, guide to creating, 122-152
Reading (see Trope)
Symbols, Ark, aron, breast
plate, Torah crown and bells,
Torah cover, white cover,
wooden rollers, eitz chayim,
pointer, yad (See Symbols)
Translations, 128-129
Transliteration, Aramaic, Hebrew
and Yiddish
Tribe(s), tribal, tribalism, 23-27,
154
Trope (See Leyning)
Tutor(s)(ing), (See Mentor)
Twins, 32-49
Tzedakah, donations, philanthropy, 27, 42, 161, 164, 166
Tzitzit, 101-104
    blessing, 104
    ritual for tying new, 105
    (Also see Tallit)

U

Ukraine, 154-155

V

Vision Quest, (See Hitbodedut)
Vows, 22

W

Whimple, 199-200
Women, girls, female, 40, 139-
    141, 189

X

Y

Yad, pointer (See Symbols)
yad Elohim ba-kol, 192
Yarmulke, (See Kippah)

Z

Zelophehad, daughters of, 139

Made in the USA
Middletown, DE
07 October 2015